Cambridge Elements

Elements in Ancient Egypt in Context
edited by
Gianluca Miniaci
University of Pisa
Juan Carlos Moreno García
CNRS, Paris
Anna Stevens
University of Cambridge and Monash University

IMMIGRATION AND BORDERS IN ANCIENT EGYPT

Danielle Candelora
College of the Holy Cross

Shaftesbury Road, Cambridge CB2 8EA, United Kingdom

One Liberty Plaza, 20th Floor, New York, NY 10006, USA

477 Williamstown Road, Port Melbourne, VIC 3207, Australia

314–321, 3rd Floor, Plot 3, Splendor Forum, Jasola District Centre, New Delhi – 110025, India

Cambridge University Press is part of Cambridge University Press & Assessment, a department of the University of Cambridge.

We share the University's mission to contribute to society through the pursuit of education, learning and research at the highest international levels of excellence.

www.cambridge.org
Information on this title: www.cambridge.org/9781009500128

DOI: 10.1017/9781009500111

© Danielle Candelora 2026

This publication is in copyright. Subject to statutory exception and to the provisions of relevant collective licensing agreements, no reproduction of any part may take place without the written permission of Cambridge University Press & Assessment.

When citing this work, please include a reference to the DOI 10.1017/9781009500111

First published 2026

A catalogue record for this publication is available from the British Library

A Cataloging-in-Publication data record for this Element is available from the Library of Congress

ISBN 978-1-009-50012-8 Hardback
ISBN 978-1-009-50013-5 Paperback
ISSN 2516-4813 (online)
ISSN 2516-4805 (print)

Cambridge University Press & Assessment has no responsibility for the persistence or accuracy of URLs for external or third-party internet websites referred to in this publication and does not guarantee that any content on such websites is, or will remain, accurate or appropriate.

For EU product safety concerns, contact us at Calle de José Abascal, 56, 1°, 28003 Madrid, Spain, or email eugpsr@cambridge.org

Immigration and Borders in Ancient Egypt

Elements in Ancient Egypt in Context

DOI: 10.1017/9781009500111
First published online: March 2026

Danielle Candelora
College of the Holy Cross

Author for correspondence: Danielle Candelora, dcandelora@holycross.edu

Abstract: The aim of this Element is to explore borders in ancient Egypt – both the territorial and ideological boundaries of the state as well as the divisions such lines draw between 'Egyptians' and 'Others.' Despite the traditional understanding of ancient Egypt as an insular society isolated by its borders, many foreigners settled in Egypt over the course of the longue durée, significantly impacting its culture. After examining the applicability of territorial state borders to the ancient world, the boundaries of ancient Egypt are investigated, questioning how they were defined, when, and by whom. Then a framework is presented for considering the reflexive ontological relationship between borders and immigrants, grappling with how identity is affected by elements like geography, the state, and locality. Finally, case studies are presented that critically examine ancient Egypt's northern, eastern, western and southern 'borders' and the people who crossed them.

Keywords: Ancient Egypt, immigration, borders, identity, foreigners

© Danielle Candelora 2026

ISBNs: 9781009500128 (HB), 9781009500135 (PB), 9781009500111 (OC)
ISSNs: 2516-4813 (online), 2516-4805 (print)

Contents

1 Introduction: Lines in the Sand   1

2 B/ordering   6

3 Othering: Borders and Identity   23

4 Borderlands and Immigration   35

5 Borderland Identities   46

6 Conclusions: Immigrant Impacts   57

   Works Cited   60

1 Introduction: Lines in the Sand

The study of ancient borders – from the definition of the term to the research questions and conclusions – is fundamentally predicated on the interests of the scholar. If one is interested in fixed, even fortified, geopolitical boundaries tied to sovereign power, these can be found in state propagandistic texts as well as in the archaeological remains of Hadrian's Wall, the Great Wall of China, and the Second Cataract forts of ancient Egypt's Nubian frontier, to name just a few examples. This delineation of power can also be expressed symbolically, as in the case of Rome's *pomerium* line, which despite having strong effects on law, *imperium*, and cultural practice was not a physical reality. The common historical or literary vignette of drawing a line in the sand, such as Gaius Popillius Laenas drawing a line around Seleucid Emperor Antiochus IV to prevent his invasion of Egypt (Livy, *Ab Urbe Condita*, XLV.12 & Polybius, *Histories*, XXIX.27), is another example of the power of figurative borders. If one's focus is on the religious or ideological roles of borders, these can be seen in ancient civilizations including Egypt, Rome, Sumer, and the Maya, which performed rituals involving the walking, measuring, or plowing of the border (Diener & Hagen 2012, pp. 24–30). Religious complexes often had sacred boundaries to separate the pure from the profane, and religious references abound of cosmic borders or the role of the gods in securing the territorial borders of the terrestrial king or state. In these cases, it naturally follows that borders would be defined as fixed limits, whether real or metaphorical, set lines that were often marked on the landscape and whose main role was to divide, delineating territory, population, polities, and even purity. In the end, we are left with a neat patchwork map with distinct sections abutting along clear edges, distinguishing what was, for instance, Egypt versus Nubia, who was an Israelite versus a Philistine, or a Roman versus a Celt.

Conversely, for those interested in the lived reality of the border, such rigid lines become much more blurred. Archaeological, textual, and art historical evidence from a more local scale consistently presents borders as zones rather than lines, porous and flexible, with overlapping cultural inputs that result in new, hybrid production. Seals from Kanesh showed both blending and maintenance in Anatolian and Assyrian motifs, serving as identity markers reflecting generational shifts in multiethnic families (Larsen & Lassen 2014). At Fort Ross in California, Indigenous Californian women utilized their own traditional cooking practices to produce meals that were more familiar to their Alutiiq husbands (Lightfoot *et al.* 1998; Lightfoot & Martinez 1995). Women in Roman Pannonia (Rothe 2014, pp. 508–511) and Egyptian Nubia (Smith 2013, pp. 88–94) preserved traditional, local burial styles while others melded cultural inputs from both local and imperial customs.

Everything from religion and technology to daily basics such as foodways and dress was adapted and transformed in these borderland regions. Even in the case of fortified, walled borders, it is possible to examine both the efficacy of the fortifications as well as the exchange and mobility that occurred in spite of those defenses. The study of borders therefore invites – or demands – that we become more comfortable with ambiguity and accept that different conceptions of borders can exist simultaneously at distinct scales or to individual actors. We need to extend Frankfort's "multiplicity of approaches" in accepting contradictions in the Egyptian religious realm (Frankfort 1948, pp. 4, 18–19) to their ideas of borders as well. It was likely conceivable to the ancient Egyptian, without much effort, to have rigid, impermeable borders established by the king and the gods while simultaneously recognizing that those borders were crossed constantly by people, goods, and ideas.

In both cases, it is clear that borders are fundamentally linked to questions of identity, belonging, and group inclusion. Borders dictate not only what territory may lie under whose sovereignty, but who is permitted to live or belong in that territory, distinguishing between insider and outsider (Agnew 1994, p. 63; Biersteker & Weber 1996, pp. 2–3; Doty 1996, p. 128; Murphy 1996, p. 97; Paasi 2018, pp. 23–24; Shachar 2019, p. 98). It is precisely the border that determines who is a "citizen" or a foreigner who has had to cross into the host land, meaning there is an inextricable ontological relationship between borders and immigrants. Barth first argued that ethnic groups themselves were defined more by their boundaries than the "cultural stuff that it encloses" (Barth 1969, p. 15), suggesting that the relationship between borders and collective identity is mutually constitutive.

The link between territory and identity has an unconscious but strong homogenizing effect, eliding the diversity within territorial boundaries in favor of a shared self-conception based on place, and rendering that collective identity coterminous with the edges of the polity (Agnew 1994, pp. 56, 70–71; Paasi 2013, pp. 478–482, 2020; Smith 2016, pp. 1–3; Van Houtum & Van Naerssen 2002, p. 126). Paasi defines this as socio-spatial fetishism, noting that "physical and symbolic borders and b/orderings are critical in the social construction of otherness" as well as a national identity (Paasi 2020, p. 21). Terms like "immigrant" and "alien" inherently reference a normative collective identity to which these elements do not belong (Doty 1996, p. 128). This homogenizing tendency has already been noted in the study of ancient Egypt; in 2006, Kemp wrote that "Books about ancient Egypt take for granted that the ancient Egyptians were already, in essence, a nation" (Kemp 2006, p. 19), and that the Egyptians had a shared word for humankind (*rmṯ*), which referred to their collectivity as a people, excluding foreigners (Kemp 2006, pp. 22–23; Kootz 2013, p. 34). This idea was seemingly reified in Egyptian ideology, in which cosmic order (*ma'at*), represented by *kmt*, the arable land of the Nile Valley, as well as its inhabitants, was diametrically opposed to *isfet* or chaos, embodied in foreigners, foreign lands, and the desert (*dšrt*) (Assmann 2003, pp. 151–153; Loprieno 1988; Zivie-Coche 2018, pp. 25–26). Indeed, Assmann argues that, in this worldview, foreigners cannot be considered human at all (Assmann 2003, pp. 152–153). This conception of the world ordered by clear cultural and geographic borders reflects modern understandings of nation-states, political sovereignty within territory, and "ideologies of cultures as hermetically sealed and spatially fixed" (Paasi 2013, p. 478), rather than lived realities – whether in ancient Egypt or today.

Egypt is perhaps one of the most alluring of ancient civilizations in which to find absolute borders because of the uniqueness of its geography (Figure 1). Its "natural" borders fall in the north at the Mediterranean Sea, in the east at the Red Sea, in the west at the impassable expanse of desert, and in the south at the First Cataract of the Nile (Hornung 1992, p. 74; S.T. Smith 2005, p. 209). These rigid geographical features allow us to envision a state that was neat and nearly square, and they give rise to the extremely pervasive misconception of a unitary Egyptian identity isolated within those borders (Zivie-Coche 2018, p. 25). State texts reinforce this vision and contrast it with wretched foreigners and even the foreign lands themselves, whose physical features are opposite to Egypt's own. Yet Egypt was never really isolated, and immigrants from numerous places can be found settling in and integrating into Egypt across the *longue durée* (Schneider 2010; Taterka 2024). Reconciling these two conflicting understandings of Egypt, characterized by Loprieno as *topos* and *mimesis* (Loprieno 1988), requires the investigation of multiple forms of evidence, as well as a willingness to accept multiple simultaneous conceptions of ancient Egypt's borders. Furthermore, it is crucial to remember that the location, permeability, and understanding of borders, as well as their attitudes toward immigrants, certainly changed often over the millennia of Egypt's history.

1.1 Previous Approaches

The study of borders and immigration by necessity must embrace every available modality of evidence, from textual to archaeological, imperial to individual, and international to local. The most well-known and often discussed textual sources are the royal inscriptions denigrating foreigners and the so-called border stelae, which are often the same texts. Textual evidence on borders and

Figure 1 Map of ancient Egypt and Nubia, by author.

immigration, however, can also be found in literary tales, graffiti, personal letters, religious texts, and more. The archaeological record is crucial to understanding the reality of border experiences in sites like border fortresses as well as settlements in which locals and immigrants lived together; often archaeology provides our only evidence for immigration or cultural encounters.

Most studies on borders in ancient Egypt have investigated the topic from the political and/or ideological perspective. Examinations often focus on the definition of the ancient Egyptian terms *tȝš* and *ḏrw*, including to what extent these terms can be compared to modern notions of borders (Galán 1995, pp. 102–103; Siegel 2022), or on ancient Egyptian political thought on the nature of *ma'at* and *isfet* and its reflection in Egypt's border policies (Langer 2018; Langer & Fernández-Götz 2020, pp. 39–41). Many concentrated on the precise extent of those borders (Schlott-Schwab 1981) and on the nature of the political control exerted by the Egyptian state within or beyond them. Interpretations range from rigid pharaonic sovereign control over the Nile Valley, deserts, and imperial holdings beyond, to recognizing that these claims of established borders may only indicate the possibility of the king asserting his influence, whether via violence or simply a trade arrangement (Bleiberg 1984; Darnell 2007; Galán 1995, 1999; Hornung 1992; Koozz 2013; Liverani 1990, 2001; Lorton 1974; Morris 2004, 2017; Müller-Wollermann 1996; Quirke 1988; Redford 1992; Schlott-Schwab 1981; Siegel 2022; Smith 1995, 2005b; Török 2008; Vogel 2011; Zibelius-Chen 1988; Zivie-Coche 2018).

The study of foreigners in ancient Egypt has also been worked on extensively. Earlier approaches focused on culture-historical definitions of foreign identities and the rapidity of their complete assimilation to Egyptian cultural norms – their Egyptianization. More recent scholarship addresses the biases inherent in the concept of Egyptianization and investigates how the identities of foreigners were adapted, transformed, or maintained when they moved to Egypt (Candelora 2022a; Matić 2020; Schneider 2010; Taterka 2024). Interestingly, there is a tendency, even in recent scholarship, to continue to refer to these individuals as (acculturated) foreigners rather than using the term "immigrants." While some people were certainly brought to Egypt against their will, many moved voluntarily, and all would be referred to in modern parlance as some variety of migrant. Indeed, many of these individuals maintained and advertised their foreignness as a strategy to promote their craft or professional specialty (Candelora 2019a), but the continued use of the term "foreigner" implies that they never quite lose their foreign status to scholars, despite seemingly having done so in the eyes of their ancient neighbors. Applying modern approaches to immigration allows us to incorporate new theoretical frameworks, especially to better conceptualize the generations that came after the initial move to Egypt. Though the term "immigrant" still qualifies these individuals as distinct from natives, it at least indicates that they have made Egypt their home permanently and need to be thought of as constituting a portion of the Egyptian population and contributing to its culture.

Therefore, to study immigration/immigrants is to prioritize the *social* history and lived experience of the border, rather than solely examining the geopolitics of the border and lines on a map. Concentrating on immigrants allows us to relocate the border as the center, as well as divorcing it from its geographic constraints, to explore the border's role in the creation of new cultural products and the construction of identities. Although we can never truly understand the actual experience of ancient peoples, the attempt to reconstruct aspects of that reality from several viewpoints allows us to start to shed our own cultural frameworks to at least imagine different ways in which they might have encountered their worlds. This Element therefore approaches these entangled questions of borders and immigrants in ancient Egypt from the perspective of ambiguity, embracing the likelihood of a multiplicity of understandings that changed over time.

2 B/ordering

Borders are most often conceived of as lines on a map – edges, limits, or divisions of land. They are delimitations of space that define the geographical edges of a polity and symbolize the territory within which that polity has sovereignty (Bissonnette & Vallet 2022, p. 1). In setting those territorial and political boundaries, borders also mark the distinction between the interior and exterior, those who belong and the "Other" (Newman 2003, pp. 5–6). This encompasses notions of citizenship and the legal rights such membership confers, requiring some form of control to supervise entry not only into the territorial space of the state but also into its citizenry (Diener & Hagen 2012, p. 86; Shachar 2019). Modern borders are marked in the physical world by border control stations, walls, and even signage, and are monitored and policed. Especially since 9/11, borders around the world have been fortified, with more than eighty walls constructed as of 2018 (Paasi 2022, pp. 7–9; Vallet 2022, p. 7). This increasing level of control and surveillance of conflicted borders is juxtaposed strikingly with what many scholars are describing as a move toward a borderless world, one in which modern technology, communication and trade networks, and mobility are effectively erasing many of the world's borders (Diener & Hagen 2012, pp. 60–61; Paasi 2018). Yet legal scholars argue that borders are not disappearing, but being reinvented through forms of border control that have been unlinked from territorial boundaries, while the legal privileges of citizenship are still inextricably bound to the lines drawn on the map (Shachar 2019, pp. 96–98). Even the study of borders has traditionally been limited to disciplines like political science and geography, so embedded are the notions of borders and territorial sovereignty (Mullin 2011a, p. 12).

Yet this concept of the border is a relatively modern invention. Numerous studies have shown that the idea of borders as state limits was "invented" with the signing of the Treaties of Westphalia at the end of the Thirty Years' War (Diener & Hagen 2012, p. 3; Shachar 2019, pp. 97–98). Essentially, these treaties were agreements to limit state power through the partition of space, but gave rise to, as Amilhat Szary put it, "a long lasting tautology whereby territory is defined by state, state by sovereignty, and sovereignty by territory" (Amilhat Szary 2015, p. 4). She even notes that these early European boundary treaties are contemporaneous with the first precise regional maps that could be used to demonstrate or "prove" the location of those borders (Amilhat Szary 2015, p. 5). Krishna proposes that the modern obsession with mapping borders is a means to literally inscribe nationality and sovereignty (Krishna 1994). This Westphalian system of territorial sovereignty received its current form in the mapping out of nation-states after the world wars and the fall of the Soviet Union (Baud & Van Schendel 1997, p. 215; Langer & Fernández-Götz 2020, p. 37) and is reified in the United Nations (UN) Charter (Art. 2, Para. 4), which states that "all Members shall refrain in their international relations from the threat or use of force against the territorial integrity or political independence of any state" (Diener & Hagen 2012, p. 62).

Many scholars have demonstrated that this particular brand of territoriality – the concept of the sovereign state – is the "unquestioned geographical framework within which we consider any and all issues ranging from ethnicity to migration to water quality" (Murphy 1996, p. 104), and within which we approach the study of ancient states and their borders. Yet this particularly Westphalian conception of borders, aside from being modern, is also an invention. These types of clear-cut, sharp boundaries do not exist in reality, and our insistence on finding and studying them is a reflection of our own socio-spatial fetishism or cartographic anxiety (Krishna 1994; Paasi 2020, 2022, pp. 7–9; Strassoldo 1977, p. 85). Consequently, modern parallels will be explored throughout as a means to destabilize our fixed cultural understanding of borders and to introduce potential alternative perspectives that can be applied to the ancient evidence.

2.1 Blurring Borders

A brief survey quickly begins to blur this perception of borders. Borders often correspond with natural features in the landscape principally because those features actually exist in reality (Smith 2016, pp. 2–3). Otherwise, the "lines on a map" do not translate into a lived experience. Eighteenth-century European sovereigns, among many others from across history, utilized rivers and mountain chains to reinforce their power as derived from God (Amilhat Szary 2015, p. 5). Even when you construct an encounterable border on the landscape, like a border wall, it is highly permeable and unenforceable (De Leon 2015; Vallet 2022, p. 12). Many of the well-known examples from the ancient world, such as Hadrian's Wall, the Great Wall of China, the Sadd-e Sekandar, and Sumerian walls were also permeable in practice, meant more as projections of imperial power and perhaps staging grounds for campaigns than for preventing population movement (Diener & Hagen 2012, pp. 33–34; Hodgson 2017; Mojtahed-Zadeh 2005). In ancient Egypt, only a few freestanding walls existed and were also likely meant only to structure and direct mobility. Strings of border fortresses, located in the southern, northwestern, and northeastern regions, were certainly utilized for surveillance and the control or recording of population movement, as attested in the Semna Dispatches and Papryus Anastasi V (Knoblauch 2019; Kraemer & Liszka 2016; Morris 2004, pp. 804–809, 2017; Schneider 2017; Siegel 2022, pp. 15–16; Smither 1945). They were also used for organizing trade and military expeditions, and served as manifestations of the power of the Egyptian king, rather than complete blockades against migration (Siegel 2022, 2024).

Furthermore, borders need not conform to geography or territorial limits at all. One of the most common places to encounter border control checkpoints is in airports, which often sit well within the geographical interior of the state (Paasi 2013, p. 485). Ambassadors have diplomatic immunity, meaning that these individuals technically embody the border, taking it with them wherever they go, and embassies themselves exist as sovereign islands within other states (Diener & Hagen 2012, pp. 74–80). In ancient Egypt, parallels can be found in the border forts, which in the New Kingdom fell well within the claimed territorial limits of the Egyptian state or king. For instance, while royal inscriptions at Kurgus and Naharin proclaimed these as the locations of Thutmose I and Thutmose III's established borders (Davies 2017; Vogel 2011), the corresponding border forts (or checkpoints?) were located in the Sinai and at the Second Cataract hundreds of kilometers away. Several of the Amarna Letters have also been interpreted as representing versions of passports (Tarawneh 2011, p. 275, EA 30) or duty-free statements (Moran 1992, pp. 112–113, EA 39, 40), suggesting that the sovereignty of Late Bronze Age emperors could be envisioned as traveling beyond their territories.

Finally, political claims to territory do not always correspond with actual political control or sovereignty. The United States and China have planted their flags on the moon, an action synonymous with staking claim to territory (Rudnicki 2016, p. 304), and the Outer Space Treaty gives satellites and spacecraft the ability to carry sovereignty in the same way as ships or ambassadors. The UN Convention on the Law of the Sea, 1967–1982, resulted

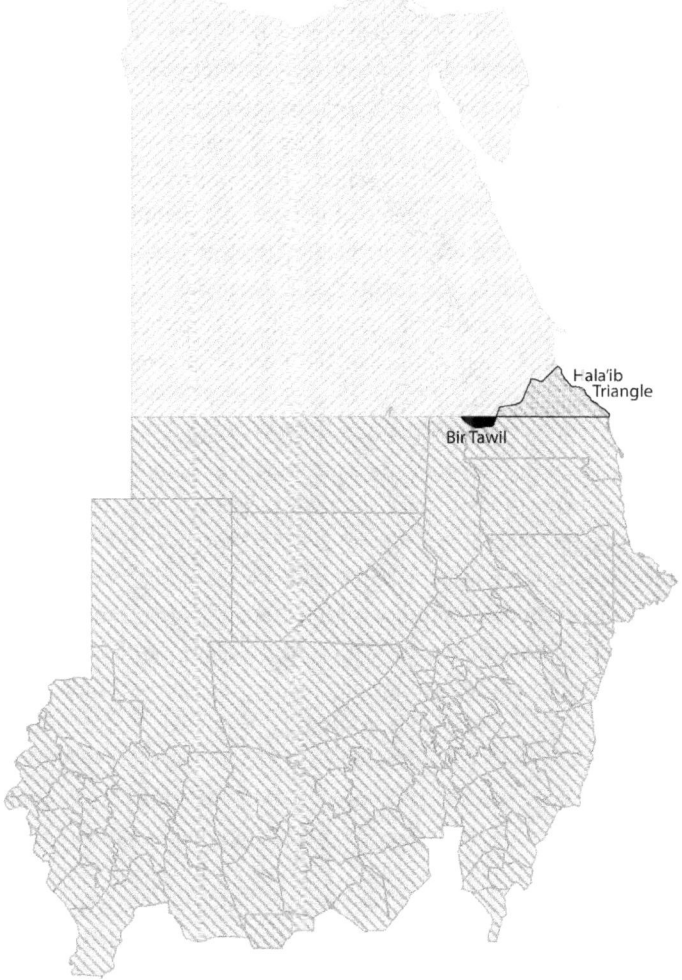

Figure 2 Bir Tawil and the Hala'ib Triangle – Cmglee McGeddon, CC BY 3.0, via Wikimedia Commons.

in legislation dictating economic, jurisdictional, and even mining rights to seabeds, often in no way geographically contiguous with the country claiming those rights. In 2007, Russia used a submersible to plant its flag and claim sovereignty over the North Pole seabed and its resources, despite not yet having the technology to exploit those resources (Diener & Hagen 2012, pp. 76–80). Terrestrial examples can also be found if the territory being claimed or disputed is either extremely difficult or undesirable to control. The contested Indo-Pakistani border at Siachen Glacier was originally left unmapped during Partition due to the hostile environment and terrain. It has since been manned by military personnel on both sides, thousands of whom have died from exposure rather than armed conflict (Krishna 1994, p. 512). Additionally, Hans Island, a 1.3 square kilometer spit of uninhabited land in the Arctic, was contested until 2022 between Canada and Denmark. Though the conflict really centered on where the water rights of each country fell, this barren island became the centerpiece of the friendly dispute (Rudnicki 2016). In contrast, Bir Tawil (Figure 2) is a 2,060 square kilometer area of desert between Sudan and Egypt, assigned to both countries by British administrative mapmakers in 1899 and 1902 respectively. Yet neither claim the territory as a strategy to boost their claims to the nearby and much more valuable Hala'ib Triangle, disorienting "our expectations of what nations and borders are trying to achieve" (Bonnett 2014, p. 76). Similar debates extend into Egyptology concerning whether the state was ever actually in control of the surrounding desert regions or oases, as well as how contested borders were navigated (Darnell 2007; Hubschmann 2010b; Morris 2010a).

Another complicating issue is entangled terminology. Academic discussions of borders often deal not only with the term "border," but also "boundary," "frontier," and "borderland," all of which share the basic definition of divisions of groups and/or geography. Other languages such as French, German, and Spanish each have a singular term that encompasses all of these associated concepts (*frontière, grenze, frontera*) (Langer 2018, pp. 48–49; Parker 2006, p. 79), while in English the distinctions between them shift by study. Both border and boundary have been defined as a linear geopolitical limit; frontier, border, and borderland as zones of interaction and exchange; borderland as the no-man's-land between two unified polities; frontiers as the regions beyond the edges of imperial systems rather than between them, etcetera (Adelman & Aron 1999; Amilhat Szary 2015, pp. 1–2; Baud & Van Schendel 1997; Feuer 2016; Langer & Fernández-Götz 2020, pp. 33–35; Newman 2003; Paasi 2022, pp. 7–9; Parker 2006; Strassoldo 1977). Yet all are spatial practices tied to territoriality, sovereignty, and identity.

2.2 New Border Studies

Recent scholarship has elucidated that geographic, political, and cultural borders are discontiguous more often than not, and that even the most fortified and surveilled of borders are quite permeable. Borders can therefore, as uncomfortable as it may seem, be divorced from notions of sovereignty or territoriality. They can overlap, change over time, and be fuzzy (Feuer 2016, p. 51; Paasi & Zimmerbauer 2016). Indeed, the study of native groups from around the world has been extremely helpful in presenting alternative models of territoriality. In North America, for example, native groups did not entertain such bounded notions of land ownership or sovereignty and had to be forced into these legal constraints by the westward expansion of the United States. Tribal groups with diverse leadership structures were assigned single leaders who were meant to embody sovereignty, and the tribe was assigned a parcel of land over which it previously had no notions of claim (Goldberg-Ambrose 1994, pp. 1130–1134). A fascinating project called Native Land Digital (https://native-land.ca) is using historical documents and ethnographic sources to reconstruct a map of Indigenous groups and languages around the world – the outcome has produced a map that defies our expectations, showing territories that overlap and areas that remain unclaimed. This project also clarifies that some relationships and overlaps are visible only at the most local of scales. This undertaking helps us visualize alternative organizations of territory that account for borders and identities that overlay one another's edges, rather than being stitched neatly together into a "patchwork," "mosaic," "jigsaw," or any number of metaphors that evoke clearly defined divisions (Langer & Fernández-Götz 2020, p. 38; Shachar 2019, p. 98). When borders are conceived of in this way, they can much more easily be seen as fluid, changeable, permeable, and in constant need of maintenance.

In New Border Studies, borders have been reconceived of as bordering processes, dynamic institutions and practices that define inclusion and exclusion between territories and/or people. They are social and political constructs that are highly context- and audience-dependent and need constant reification through surveillance, fortification, ideological rhetoric, or ritual acts (Amilhat Szary 2015, pp. 6–10; Baud & Van Schendel 1997, p. 211; Diener & Hagen 2012, pp. 1–2; Feuer 2016, pp. 14, 23, 121; Laakkonen 2020; Newman 2003; Paasi 2022, pp. 1–5; Parker 2006; Parker & Vaughan-Williams 2009). Borders are also highly performative spaces wherein different aspects of identity can be emphasized in varying contexts (Mullin 2011a, p. 19). This approach demands a bottom-up perspective focused on the actors and practices that create and maintain these divisions (Newman 2003, p. 6). It also allows us to see borders more as borderlands, middle grounds, or third spaces – cultural interfaces, broader zones wherein identity is negotiated and cultural production occurs (Anzaldúa 1987, p. 3; Baud & Van Schendel 1997; Bhabha 1994; Feuer 2016; Hämäläinen & Truett 2011; Mullin 2011a; White 1991, 2006). Instead of treating the border as peripheral, this framework treats the border as the center, at least for some of the population, and acknowledges that borders and borderlands can occur within the interior of the state as well (Baud & Van Schendel 1997, p. 212). Borders can divide territories, social groups, and even cultural practices and values, sometimes simultaneously, though often not. For example, the original Mason–Dixon Line from the 1760s marked the contested border between Pennsylvania, Maryland, and Delaware, forming a border – which was even marked on the landscape by stelae – well within the United States interior. And, although invoked as significant during (and since) the Civil War, this border did not coincide with divisions in practice between slave-owning states and free states, groups who considered themselves culturally Southern or Northern, the political division between the Union and the Confederacy, nor did it mark a boundary north of which institutional racism ceased to exist (Castronovo 1997). Borders are multilayered and deeply entangled constructs reified and reinforced through ongoing processes of demarcation and division; "borders are not 'natural' phenomena; they exist in the world only to the extent that humans regard them as meaningful" (Diener & Hagen 2012, p. 1).

2.3 Borders in Ancient Egypt

In applying these approaches to the evidence from ancient Egypt, it is important to be cognizant of the cartographic anxiety or territorial trap that allows us to see only the Westphalian borders of a sovereign state. The most commonly depicted map of ancient Egypt shows a "state-territory named Km.t" whose politico-territorial borders "coincide with the topographical ones" – namely the defined natural demarcations of the deserts, Mediterranean Sea, and First Cataract (Kootz 2013, p. 40; see also Hornung 1992; S.T. Smith 2005, 2003, p. 4). Yet New Kingdom nome lists establish the length of Egypt as measured not from the Mediterranean coast to the cataracts, but between various Delta cities (which changed depending on the time period, including Behdet, Tanis, Alexandria, and Piramesse) and Elephantine (Schlott-Schwab 1981, pp. 82–83). It has been repeatedly noted that "maps create a strong sense of the existence of borders" (Paasi & Zimmerbauer 2016, p. 80), indicating their "finality and permanence" (Diener & Hagen 2012, p. 76). The simple act of drawing those lines on a map literally inscribes and reifies the concept of ancient Egypt as a sovereign state (Amilhat Szary 2015, p. 5). However, for a culture that was certainly interested in the cartographic rendering of the world – examples exist of maps of the *duat*, a topographical map of Wadi Hammamat, progressions through landscapes, architectural plans, and more (Figure 3) (Barnard 2008; Shore 1987) – nothing resembling our expectation of a map that depicts Egypt or its territorial borders has yet been found (O'Connor 2012, p. 48). I would propose that this lack of map is the first of many hints that the ancient Egyptians had their own conceptions of territoriality and its relationship to power and identity, as distinct from

Figure 3 "Goldmine Papyrus," topographical map of Wadi Hammamat– courtesy of the Museo Egizio. CC0 1.0.

our Westphalian assumptions as the Indigenous example discussed in Section 2.2.

The textual record clearly demonstrates that Egypt had cultural concepts, *tꜣš w* and *ḏrw*, that resemble modern notions of borders. Much has been written debating the exact definitions and distinctions between these two terms, indicating a confusion similar to that seen around the use of the English terms "border," "boundary," "frontier," and "borderland." For instance, many have agreed that *tꜣš* represents the ancient Egyptian geopolitical administrative border, marking the territorial sovereignty of the king, while *ḏr* is a religious concept tied to the limits of the cosmos (Goelet 1999; Hornung 1992; Liverani 1990; Quirke 1988; Redford 1992; Schlott-Schwab 1981). Bleiberg argued that *tꜣš* has a more political orientation while *ḏrw* are specifically referring to geographical limits, and Lorton, approaching the issue from a legal standpoint, claims that *tꜣš* are religiously dictated boundaries while *ḏrw* are the geopolitical limits of foreign lands (Bleiberg 1984; Lorton 1974). Several scholars have stressed that while *tꜣš* should be interpreted as "border," it should be taken as an ideological statement of pharaonic power, not a literal marker of state territory (Kootz 2013; Langer & Fernández-Götz 2020; Smith 1995, p. 188, 2005b; Török 2008, p. 13; Vogel 2011, p. 322; Zibelius-Chen 1988, p. 200).

Galán's comprehensive examination of *tꜣš w* elucidated that they are not an exact correlate to a modern border line, demonstrating the contextual nature of their meaning (Galán 1995, p. 133). Within the Nile Valley, *tꜣš* indicated the "limit of the territory assigned to an estate, a town or a province," which are fixed and established by the king (Galán 1995, pp. 111–116, 133). Abroad, *tꜣš w* generally referred to the "king's sphere of influence," encompassing not only strongly controlled territories but also any area that may have regularly sent taxes or gifts, engaged in trade, or shared some sort of relationship with the Egyptian king (Galán 1995, pp. 117–126, 133–135, 1999, pp. 22–23). Crucially, he pointed out that "Egypt and the extension of Egypt's *tꜣš w* did not coincide in space" (Galán 1995, p. 135), undermining the elision of a unified Egypt with set territory. Galán's discussion of *ḏrw* reflects the complexity and confusion of the word. He suggests that *ḏrw* are tied to ideology and the cosmos, but are also real territories past the tꜣšw of the king that do not recognize his authority. In some cases, ḏrw seems to refer "to the population and/or the valuables on X's land," a meaning that also applies within Egypt during tax collection. Even the jar lid of Apepi associated bringing in the ḏrw of foreign lands with those lands contributing their bꜣk to him (Galán 1995, pp. 131–132, 1999, p. 25).

Recently, Siegel reconceptualized these two terms through modern border frameworks. He argued that both ḏrw and tꜣšw were boundaries, though the former were immutable while the latter could be established or changed by the king (Siegel 2022, p. 7). He nuanced Galán's notion of tꜣš, stating:

> I prefer to view a tꜣš as a royally established performance of power that demarcates space where one could *potentially* be subjected to the violent force of the pharaoh. This area did not necessarily have to be bounded in a linear fashion or even contiguous; rather, a tꜣš established a horizon wherein the Pharaonic state could levy taxes, requisition personnel, conscript or impress individuals, seize goods, engage in trade, send messengers, or inscribe itself upon the landscape in the form of monuments, fortresses, military campaigns, commercial expeditions, or ritual practice. (Siegel 2022, p. 9)

This perception of tꜣš acknowledges that borders are performative, marked by continuous action or processes of reinscription, and need not be contiguous or linear. He also made the excellent point that the very fact that we have such trouble locating or defining the tꜣšw and ḏrw of ancient Egypt "should serve as an obvious warning" that they had concepts of boundaries and political borders distinct from our own (Siegel 2022, pp. 9).

Siegel further noted that "tꜣš itself can be a verb meaning 'to delimit, to divide'" (Siegel 2022, pp. 10 n. 40, Wb V, 236:15–237:8). Conversely, ḏr is related to the compound term r-ḏr for "entire(ty)" (Wb V, 589.6–591.8), while the glyph itself (Gardiner sign M36) represents a bundle of flax stems literally encircled by rope. Perhaps the confusion between these two terms is paralleled by the association between the two ancient Egyptian conceptions of eternity, ḏt (linear time) and nḥḥ (circular time) (Assmann 2003, pp. 18–19). Our modern worldview provides no strong cultural comparisons to these differentiated ideas, demonstrating a completely alternative understanding of time. Similarly, tꜣš may be a more linear and ḏr a more circular, all-encompassing understanding of boundaries and what they contain, again indicating a unique and disparate way of defining and dividing the world.

Within the Nile Valley, the most local borders were field and estate boundaries, which, at least ideologically, were established by royal command and were meant to be fixed. Estate lands and their produce were endowed to specific cults, and the stelae recording those endowments generally mention only the field's

Figure 4 Field marker, tomb of Nebamun, Thebes – by author.

dimensions rather than location, and they were held in temples. Some of these donation texts, along with scenes from the New Kingdom Theban tombs of Nebamun (Figure 4) and Amenemopet, indicate that some regular field boundaries were marked on the land with stones or stelae, though none have been found in situ (Galán 1995, pp. 109–110, 139–142). Increasing in scale, estates, towns, and cities could have their own demarcated tꜣšw, as did the forty-two provinces (spꜣt) into which Egypt was administratively subdivided. These were also dictated by the king, and the autobiography of Khnumhotep II indicates they might also have been marked in some cases by stelae, as was the city of Amarna (Galán 1995, pp. 105, 136; Quirke 1988, pp. 262).

Although these domestic borders seem to coincide with modern notions of territorial limits, a closer examination of the sources and their contexts complicates this picture. For instance, Galán notes that only six of the Amarna stelae were truly meant to mark borders, including measurement data, while the rest were more akin to royal dedications to the Aten (Galán 1995 pp. 136–137, 145). Further, field borders were so often disputed that the Duties of the Vizier from the tomb of Rekhmire made it clear that this administrative headache was his responsibility, and Ramses II complained in his Abydos dedicatory inscription that he had to order that field boundaries be written down rather than preserved orally (Galán 1995, pp. 114–116; Siegel 2024, pp. 24). This frequency of disputes is understandable given that these field boundaries were quite literally erased from the land with the flood and had to be reestablished annually. Shore even notes how incongruous it seems, given these circumstances, that no field maps seem to have existed (Shore 1987, p. 128). In the autobiography of Khnumhotep, it seems that the Oryx nome was either so powerful or so disputed that multiple successive kings (Amenemhet I, Senwosret I, and Senwosret II) felt required to reestablish its borders, including its water rights and control of local resources like tamarisk trees. Additionally, this text indicates that the district was demarcated with stelae on its northern and southern *tȝš*, whereas its eastern and western edges ended at the *ḫȝst* (hill country) (Galán 1995, pp. 105–106). Even in the Pyramid Texts, the borders of the country are referred to as the "two mountains" (Kootz 2013, p. 40). The lack of clearly established borders in inhospitable landscapes is a common phenomenon throughout history; Greek colonies in northern Africa marked their borders along the Mediterranean coast, but not on their desert edges, while Malay and Mongol polities were much less concerned with borders overall, focusing their control on main cities and the transportation arteries connecting them (Diener & Hagen 2012, pp. 27–31).

Collectively, this evidence indicates two things: (1) that the concept of *tȝš* was fully predicated on the specific geography of the Nile Valley. Only the northern and southern nome borders required marking, and the territory of these districts seems not to have included the deserts, just settlements and arable land; (2) that the demarcation of these internal boundaries likely had less to do with ownership of territory than to whom or where the harvest or resources of said land were assigned, and who was responsible for administering that process – just as mineral and water rights can be owned separately from land today.

The issue becomes much more complex when attempting to define the borders of the state, and the role of the king and royal ideology in those bordering processes. Many texts, especially from the New Kingdom, refer to vague cosmic borders under the king's authority, like the winds, the four posts of heaven, what the sun encircles, etcetera. These titles legitimize royal authority within Egypt, where the monuments are located, and always represent territorial control as personal to the individual king, rather than to a sovereign state (Galán 1995, pp. 120–124; Hornung 1992, pp. 88–89; Liverani 1990; Siegel 2022, pp. 26–29; Smith 1997, p. 82).

Then there are the cases where the kings claim to have set their *tȝšw* at (often relatively vague) locations in foreign territory. These borders were associated with military victories and conquest, and also had to be established, maintained, or extended by each king in turn – they do not seem to have applied to the state beyond the royal person. Sometimes these foreign *tȝš* seem to be marked, either by stelae hailing the establishment of the particular king's *tȝš*, or by strings of border forts that represented real surveillance and control of population movements and trade (Dunham & Janssen 1960; Knoblauch 2019; Morris 2017; Siegel 2022, pp. 11–15; S.T. Smith 2005, p. 211; Smither 1945; Vogel 2011). However, several scholars have argued that these stelae should be seen as victory stelae commemorating specific deeds and projecting royal power, rather than functioning as literal border markers claiming ownership of territory (Eyre 1990; Galán 1995, pp. 137, 148–151; Siegel 2022, p. 12; Thum 2022). For instance, both Thutmose I and III have stelae at Kurgus (Figure 5), though the farthest southern extent of actual Egyptian control seems to have ended in the region of Gebel Barkal, some 250 kilometers downstream (Galán 1995, p. 148; S.T. Smith 2005, p. 215). Even the fortresses fall well inside the claimed *tš* of various Egyptian kings, delimiting the fertile land of the Nile Valley and Delta, rather than serving as border control for the full expanse of territory claimed by Egypt.

This raises the question of what should be considered the borders of a sovereign state called Egypt. Do these borders fall at the limits of the king's political control, his claimed *tš* in the Levant and Nubia? Or are they located at the edge of the Nile Valley, the traditional division between *ma'at* and *isfet*, between the black and red lands? Many scholars have referred to this territory, *kmt*, as "Egypt proper" (Galán 1995, p. 9; Langer 2018, p. 49; S.T. Smith 2005, p. 227), and argue that in ancient Egyptian political thought, the *ma'at/isfet* dichotomy also marked the division between Egyptian and foreign – territorially, culturally, and demographically (Assmann 1990, pp. 174–236; Langer

Figure 5 Stelae of Thutmose I (left) and Thutmose III (right), Kurgus, by author after Davies 2017, figures 6 and 7.

2018; Langer & Fernández-Götz 2020; S.T. Smith 2005, p. 228). Certainly, the *tʒš* established by Senwosret III at Semna belonged specifically to him, rather than to Egypt (Galán 1995, pp. 108–109). But early in the New Kingdom, texts began to refer to the *tʒšw* of *kmt* being located abroad. So did the ancient Egyptians conceive of themselves as living in a sovereign state known as *kmt* (Goelet 1999, p. 41; Kootz 2013, p. 40)? And did that state's authority extend beyond the Nile Valley, controlling the deserts, oases, and conquered lands, and existing separately from the king?

2.4 Bordering *kmt*

Ancient Egyptians' conceptions of their own territoriality shifted over time. Up through the First Intermediate Period, references to an entity of Egypt were often made in the dual, using the terms *tʒwy* (two lands) or titles like *nsw bjty* (king of Upper and Lower Egypt), while in some cases the incredibly vague term *tʒ pn* (this land) was used. This duality was also inherently acknowledged in ideological symbols such as the White and Red crowns and titulary such as the king's Two Ladies name, referring to both Upper and Lower Egypt (Wengrow 2006, pp. 207–215). The words *tʒš* and *drw* do not appear in Old Kingdom texts, but official titles through the Middle Kingdom do refer to doors/gates (*r-ʿ3*) or mouths (*r*) to foreign lands from the Delta or Upper Egypt (Galán 1999, pp. 27–29, 33; Kees 1934, pp. 83–86; Roccati 2015, pp. 155–159).

The terms *kmt* and *tʒ-mry* (beloved land) do not appear until the transition into the Middle Kingdom. Several graffiti in Wadi Hammamat refer to *kmt* as the place to which expeditions return, using the N23 cultivated land sign as a determinative, or juxtapose it with *dšrt*, the desert, making it clear that they were referring to the literally black, arable land of the valley. These early nonliterary examples clearly show that *kmt* was meant to indicate a type of land rather than a geopolitical entity (Galán 1999, pp. 29–36; Roccati 2015, p. 155). Middle Kingdom examples of *kmt* are much more common in literary sources such as the story of Sinuhe, Admonitions of Ipuwer, and Teachings for King Merikare, which were likely edited numerous times throughout Egyptian history. In these texts, *kmt* generally appears in opposition to foreigners or the desert, suggesting that it could have indicated a unitary sense of "Egypt," the fertile land, or both (Candelora 2022b, pp. 240–241; Galán 1999, pp. 36–41). Interestingly, this double meaning is confirmed when the internal borders of Egypt are considered; the autobiography of Khnumhotep notes that the eastern and western sides of his district extend only to the *ḫʒst*, suggesting that pharaonic state control and the sense of what constituted Egypt extended only to where the desert cliffs rose on either side of the Nile (Kootz 2013, p. 40).

Certainly, individual uses of the term *kmt* are highly variable, suggesting that their nuance was context-dependent. The stela of Senwosret I's vizier, Montuhotep, calls him *ḥry tp n kmtwt dšrwt* (Overseer of the Black Lands and Red Lands). *kmt* appears here in the plural, so it cannot refer to a single sovereign entity and is juxtaposed with the deserts in order to highlight its intended meaning of fertile lands (Goelet 1999, pp. 33–34). Another truly unique example from the Hymns to Senwosret III uses *kmt* with the people-group determinative, just like the famous example from the Victory Stele of Merenptah. Yet the use of the singular feminine pronoun to refer back to *kmt* in the following line indicates that it does not mean "Egyptians." Instead, the use of *kmt* in conjunction with *dšrt*, *tʒwy*, and *idbwy* suggests that *kmt* here is the (in this case personified) fertile land, rather than a polity or nation (Goelet 1999, pp. 36–37). A stele of Montuemhat, an official under Senwosret III, found at Semna records the title "*rʒ-ʒ ḥr kmt*" (doorway for *kmt*) (Goelet 1999, p. 33), perhaps referring to the fortress itself as the new gateway to Egypt, consequently relocating the border to the Second Cataract and confirming the king's establishment of his *tʒš* in the same location. Alternatively, because the fertile floodplain widens north of Semna, this title might imply that the black land was now considered to extend further south.

This context-dependent variability continues through the Second Intermediate Period and early New Kingdom. For instance, in a famous passage from the First Kamose Stele, the king bemoans that he has to share *kmt* with an *ʒmw* and a Nubian, a comment that already raises interesting questions about the territorial control of Kerma at the time. Yet his council's immediate response is that as far as Cusae "it is *ʒmw* waters" (*mk mw pw n ʒm.w*) and "He (Apepi) has the land of the *ʒmw*, we have *kmt*" (*ḥr=s sw ḥr tʒ n ʒm.w twɜnn ḥr kmt*) (Candelora 2020, pp. 110, 305–306). Here it appears that Kamose thought of *kmt* as the stretch of fertile land from the Delta to Upper Egypt, while his council simultaneously considered *kmt* to be whatever area the king controlled at that time, in this case only a portion of Upper Egypt south of Cusae. The near-contemporary autobiography of Ahmose, son of Ibana, notes that after the defeat of Avaris, the fighting continued to the south in *kmt* (Sethe 1927, ln. 11), implying that this Delta city was not in *kmt* (Candelora 2022b, pp. 242–243).

Even much later into the New Kingdom, sources reveal specifically contextualized uses of the term with implications for the conception of Egypt and the borders of the state. A late Twentieth Dynasty series of letters between Tjaroy and his son Butehamun reveal that neither of them conceived of Nubia, a territory controlled by the Egyptian state and by this point in history subjected to centuries of colonization, as part of *kmt* (Candelora 2022b, p. 243; Černý 1939, letters 29, 50; Wente 1990, pp. 189, 196). In a letter found at Deir el-Medina, workman's wife Takhentyshepse complains to her sister Iyt that her husband does not think her family supplies their household with enough provisions, and insists that she go down to *kmt* (McDowell 1999, p. 42n16). Again, this suggests that Deir el-Medina was not located in *kmt*, in this case certainly referring only to the fertile agricultural land, but calling into question the assumption that *kmt* was unequivocally the name for the Egyptian state.

Furthermore, there are numerous examples of places we assume to have been part of the state of Egypt that do not appear to be located in *kmt* in the ancient sources. The late Dynasty 11 examples from Wadi Hammamat that mention returning to or coming from *kmt* signify that the authors of those texts did not situate this important, resource-rich region in *kmt*. Officials' stelae and literary tales like the Eloquent Peasant provide parallel cases for the Wadi Natrun and Serabit el Khadim, and Tallet has convincingly identified the Red Sea port of Ayn Soukhna as the *ḫ3st ꜥ3mw* from the autobiography of Pepinakht (Candelora 2022b, pp. 241–242; Goelet 1999, pp. 32–33; Parkinson 2012, pp. 26, 29; Tallet 2009, pp. 712–714). Taken together, these examples demonstrate that locations that were claimed to be under the king's authority were not considered part of *kmt* – making it unlikely that *kmt* was the name for a sovereign state of Egypt in this period.

2.5 Egypt's Borders

However, a substantive change did take place under the New Kingdom imperial expansion – the concepts of *t3šw* and *kmt* came together for the first time. While Senwosret III famously boasted about expanding his borders in his Semna and Uronarti stelae, the *t3š* strictly belonged to him rather than to Egypt. The earliest example of *swsḫ t3šw kmt* (extending the borders of *kmt*), occurs in the autobiography of Ahmose, son of Ibana, in the section dedicated to Amenhotep I's Nubian campaigns (Sethe 1961, p. 7 ln. 24–25). In his Abydos stele, Thutmose I claims that he "made the *t3šw* of *t3-mry* as far as what the sun-disc encircles" and "I caused *kmt* to be on top, every land being its servant" (Galán 1995, p. 119 ex. B; Sethe 1961, pp. 102, 9–15). However, all of these examples are ideologically charged, meant to emphasize the power of the individual king in performing these great deeds. Seigel notes that most instances referring to the *t3šw kmt* or *swsḫ kmt* seem to coincide with propagandistic attempts to build cohesive shared identity and rally support against enemies, such as the Hyksos or Sea Peoples (Siegel 2022, pp. 26–27).

One of the central tenets of these New Kingdom *t3šw* is that they have to be reestablished by each successive king, again suggesting they are tied to the specific ruler rather than a state. This practice is reflected in the Amarna Letters, in which countries are referred to as belonging to specific leaders, and the international trade and diplomatic agreements must be redrawn with each new reign (Siegel 2022, pp. 26–29). Furthermore, the *tзšw* themselves encompassed vague cosmic limits or broad regions rather than having identifiable, fixed locations on the landscape (Galán 1995, p. 133). Certainly, the numerous examples of vassals gone rogue in the Amarna Letters demonstrate that the claiming or establishment of *tзšw* did not necessarily coincide with political control (Morris 2010b; Siegel 2024, p. 23). This, as well as the questionable level of control exerted by the state over the deserts, ties into alternative understandings of territorial sovereignty in which the state is viewed less as a "homogenous blob" (M.L. Smith 2007, p. 31) and more as a network with main population centers connected by corridors, and control that can be non-contiguous (M.L. Smith 2005).

For instance, on Hatshepsut's Karnak obelisks, she claimed that "Amun has caused that I rule *kmt* and *dšrt* (the black land and the red land).... He has made my *tзš* as far as the *drw* of heaven" and "*kmt, dšrt, hзswt nb(t)* (the black land, red land, and every foreign land) are united under my feet." In this example, as well as many others, all of the territorial units representative of the Egyptian worldview (*kmt, dšrt, hзswt*) are identified as separate entities that are united under the power of the king, meaning *kmt* is again unlikely to be the name of the sovereign state, but instead the designation of a type of land. She goes on to list the location of her *tзšw* (again they belong to her, not Egypt) in the four cardinal directions, and all are described as being almost mythical, or at the very least very distant, locations. Her western *tзš* is at Manu, the mythological mountain where Re sets in the evening, and her southern *tзš* is in Punt (Sethe 1961, pp. 372, 3–12). Hatshepsut did not set her border at Punt in the modern sense; she did not have both control of and claim to all territory up to Punt. It is listed here as another example of an extremely distant land, so an ideological projection of Hatshepsut's power rather than a realistic, geographic description of her or Egypt's sovereignty (Galán 1995, p. 134; Siegel 2022, p. 16)

Because so many of the modern assumptions about borders and territorial sovereignty were born via treaty, it is crucial to examine ancient treaties for these same ideas. The so-called Kuruštama treaty, dating potentially to the reign of Thutmose III or Amenhotep II, is preserved in several fragments as well as referenced in later Hittite texts. The agreement was struck between unnamed Hittite and Egyptian kings, and the extant portions refer to the relocation of the Kuruštama people, formerly Hittite subjects, to Egypt (Vigo 2024, pp. 122–123). Though our knowledge of this diplomatic document is incredibly fragmentary, no discussion of the borders between Egypt and Hatti is preserved.

Figure 6 Treaty of Qadesh, Karnak Temple, Luxor – Olaf Tausch, CC BY 3.0, via Wikimedia Commons.

The Treaty of Qadesh (Figure 6), dating from the reign of Ramses II, has survived largely intact. Remarkably, however, in a treaty that essentially focuses on a border conflict between the Egyptian and Hittite Empires, there is only one mention of the word tȝš in a standard royal epithet of Ramses II, and no indication that the two parties agreed upon an actual location for the disputed border (Kitchen 1970, p. 227 ln. 5). Instead, the agreement for peace is made between the two rulers, as was the custom in the Amarna Letters. Most importantly, the text goes on to reference that the peace will last between generations of the rulers' descendants, and finally between "the land of *kmt* with the land of Hatti, in peace and brotherhood just like us for eternity" (Kitchen 1970, pp. 227–228 ln. 13). I would argue that this is the first time we see *kmt* potentially representing a sovereign political entity separate from the king, though still crucially lacking clearly defined geopolitical borders. Yet interestingly, though the treaty goes on to outline further aspects of the agreement in language familiar from modern international relations, including trespassing, extradition rights, diplomatic immunity, mutual defense, etcetera, these arrangements are once more made specifically between Ramses and Hatusilli rather than their countries in perpetuity – suggesting again that the ancient Egyptians had a completely different understanding of territorial sovereignty.

Significantly, even the ancient Egyptians recognized their amorphous borders. The first Upper Egyptian nome was called *tꜣ sty* (Nubian land), while an area of the Western Delta was *ḫꜣsi tmḥw* (foreign/hill land of the Tjemehu) (Moreno García 2015, p. 75; Smith 1991, p. 124); in fact, this part of the Delta might not even have been considered to be *kmt*, given that it was referred to as *ḫꜣst*. The southernmost districts were included in the same administrative divisions as Lower Nubia, and the oases always received the *ḫꜣst* sign determinative, even in periods when the Egyptian kings claimed them as part of their dominion (Gauthier 1925, pp. 202–203; Smith 1997, p. 82). Therefore, we should break from trying to inscribe modern notions of linear borders and sovereign territory onto ancient Egypt, and consider that ancient Egyptians had their own conceptions of territoriality and power. Instead, we can investigate the lived reality of Egyptian borders by approaching them as border*lands* – amorphous zones where bordering practices not only created and maintained social difference but also often caused those differences to blur – and that these bordering practices could potentially distinguish people from disparate regions within Egypt more strongly than from groups across the border

3 Othering: Borders and Identity

Territoriality and borders are active forces in constructing our sense of self and the "other" (Diener & Hagen 2012, pp. 12–13; Newman 2003, p. 5). Yet it is not the border as a geopolitical line that acts as an anthropomorphized agent, but rather the practices and processes used to enculturate individual and collective identities based on bounded space (Paasi 2020; Parker 2006). These practices can be produced or reproduced via "material and ideological, conceptual and cartographic, imaginary and actual, and social and aesthetic" means (Paasi 2022, pp. 2–3), from flags to languages, state signs and slogans to local cuisines and dress. Collective identities often construct and reify themselves by emphasizing characteristics specific to a location (Paasi & Zimmerbauer 2016, p. 88), and the multiscalar nature of such bordering practices is apparent, spanning from local high school sports rivalries to international geopolitical alliances such as the Allied or Axis Powers of World War II. Identity and borders are so entangled as to be conceptually similar in many ways – both are flexible social constructs that define belonging and are reified via processes and practices that are contextual, often performative, and can be elective, imposed, or ingrained. Already in the 1960s, Barth recognized that it is through the construction of a boundary that we create and inscribe "otherness" and therefore define and maintain a sense of self (Barth 1969).

3.1 Borders and Collective Identity

This entanglement applies not only at the personal or local scale but also at the level of the state. Historically, borders have been seen as geographical markers of political sovereignty that divide polities, but also enclose national identities (Bissonnette & Vallet 2022, p. 1). Yet these national identities are *imagined* communities, conceived of as "inherently limited and sovereign," though still powerful in eliciting deep attachments (Anderson 2006, pp. 4–7). They are created by state discourse that glosses over regionality and heterogeneity (Agnew 1994; Doty 1996; Van Houtum & Van Naerssen 2002, p. 126). Our modern conception of nationality, the "idea of congruence between a people with shared characteristics and the spatial expression of their political organization," is a new idea that was also forged after Westphalia, especially during the 1800s in Europe (Smith 2016, p. 1). This notion also "assumes that the territorial state functions as a geographical container ... in which *state* borders are regarded as coincident with *political* or *social* borders" (Paasi 2013, p. 482; also see Agnew 1994; Smith 2016, pp. 5–7). This conflation of the nation and the state has led to a preconception that a unified national identity can exist and is tied to a specific location (Murphy 1996, p. 97).

The crucial role of performance as one of the bordering processes that manufactures national identity is made apparent in the daily "Retreat Ceremony" at the Wagah–Attari border between Pakistan and India (Figure 7). The ceremony takes place in a literal no-man's-land between the two countries flanked by gates painted in the colors of each country's flags. At sunset, the gates are opened and soldiers from each nation, bedecked in ceremonial uniforms and bearing their flags, march in to perform dance-like drills and shake hands. National anthems are played, and masters of ceremony on both sides of the border compete to get spectators to shout patriotic slogans more loudly than the other. Thus this border is

Figure 7 Lowering of the flag ceremony at Wagah–Attari border – Guilhem Vellut, CC BY 2.0, via Wikimedia Commons.

a physical marker on the landscape indicating where the states of India and Pakistan begin and end, but the ceremony itself also serves to create and amplify national identities in a conflicted border region (Parciack 2018; Purewal 2003).

Another process that draws boundaries not only along state lines, but also amongst identities, is determining the conditions of citizenship (Biersteker & Weber 1996, pp. 13–14). Citizenship conveys rights of access to particular spaces, as well as the attendant rights and protections that apply within that space (El-Enany 2020, p. 2; Shachar 2019, p. 98). This gives the state the authority and "ability, in the face of ambiguity and uncertainty, to impose fixed and stable meanings about who belongs and who does not belong to the nation" (Doty 1996, p. 122). Even the use of terms like "alien," "immigrant," or "refugee" indicates that these individuals are something other than the "normative citizen," a concept that would be meaningless without these outsiders or the borders that define them (Doty 1996, pp. 126–128).

Yet several theorists have demonstrated that the collective identity known as a "nation" often does not correspond to the territorial state (Agnew 1994; Newman 2002). Paasi identified around 200 states/countries globally, while arguing that there are more than 500 discernable nations, showing that multiple collective identities often exist within the borders of a single state, and can transcend them as well (Paasi 2013, p. 483). Diasporic communities, for example, share collective identities that are still often tied to but occur beyond a specific territory (Gilroy 1997, pp. 319–321; Hall 1994; Newman 2002). In this sense, linear borders are myopic constructs that tell us very little about reality and lived experience. Instead, "to focus on boundaries means to become aware of the fuzziness of social systems and groups" (Strassoldo 1977, p. 86). Another representative example is found along the imposed border between Bangladesh and northeastern India, where in some cases, the new border was established running directly through extended family compounds. Both the families and the border control forces involved complained about the arbitrariness of the division, both in territory and national identity, arguing that people on both sides shared blood, a language, clothing, cultural practices, etcetera, and that daily cross-border visits and even marriages continued in spite of the new fence (Krishna 1994, p. 515). Interestingly, the aforementioned Wagah–Attari "retreat ceremony" now features daily instances of migration – the third stage of the ceremony includes citizens and their belongings crossing the border in both directions, a standard administrative occurrence at a border crossing point that is intentionally timed to be viewed by a large audience (Parciack 2018, p. 761). This public display of access serves to highlight the permeability of the border and population mobility, and reflects the imposed nature of this border on a local population whose ties cross it.

3.2 Bordering "Egyptian-ness"

One of the most enduring Egyptological "fictions" is that of a unified, Egyptian national identity that coincides with the state's territorial borders (Zivie-Coche 2018 p. 26; also see Loprieno 2001, p. 69; Moers 2015, pp. 693–694). For instance, Hubschman writes, "The community of ancient Egypt comprised peoples who shared a common language and culture, who were ruled by a divine royal lineage and who occupied rigidly-defined territories centred around the Nile Valley and Delta regions" (Hubschmann 2010b, p. 51). However, much of the ideology of a unified Egypt was developed during the Predynastic Period to codify and support burgeoning Egyptian kingship (Wengrow 2006). This pan-Egyptian identity is often referred to using the term *rmṯ*, meaning "humankind," to indicate only Egyptians rather than foreigners (Haring 2005, pp. 164–165; Kemp 2006, pp. 22–23). Some even argue that the understanding of only Egyptians as human shows their conceived centrality in the world, their equation with order, and even a strong sense of ethnocentrism and xenophobia (Assmann 2003, p. 154; Graeff 2008; Kootz 2013, p. 34). However, recently several studies have demonstrated that *rmṯ* can in fact be used to refer to foreigners as well as Egyptians, and that a closer translation might be "people" (Candelora 2022b, pp. 244–245; Chantrain 2019; Kilani 2015; Moers 2005; Taterka 2024, pp. 116–117).

The term *tꜣ-mry,* beloved land, for the whole of Egypt has also been suggested to show a strong emotional tie between Egyptians and their "homeland" (see, for example, Matić 2020, p. 6). It should be noted that this loaded term does not appear until the Middle Kingdom, and mostly occurs in propagandistic literary texts that mainly employ it to juxtapose Egypt with foreign lands (Goelet 1999, pp. 29–30). In some instances, *kmt* also seems to have evoked attachment. In the Satire of the Trades, also composed during the Middle Kingdom, the trader/messenger who has gone abroad only knows himself again when he returns to *kmt* (P. Sallier II, column VII, ln. 6–8). Yet Moers aptly notes that "it is by no means clear, however, whether this passage is on Egypt as a political (vulgo: 'national') entity or for example just about 'landscape,' to name just one possible alternative" (Moers 2015, p. 699). Another alternative would be that the trader recognizes himself upon returning to his home – the very next line in the text describes him reaching his house in the evening (Simpson 2003, p. 434). A similar nuance might be found in the late Twentieth Dynasty letters between Butehamun and his father, Tjaroy, who was stationed in Nubia. In multiple letters, both express their desire for Tjaroy to return to *kmt* from the "far-off land" (Wente 1990, p. 189 L. 312) but specify they mean his return home to Thebes and to the "gods of your town" (Wente 1990, p. 196 L. 317; see also Černý 1939, L. 29, 50).

Furthermore, specific hometowns are emphasized in highly propagandistic texts such as the Hymns to Senwosret III. While this collection of hymns is usually discussed as celebrating the king's role in securing and protecting a unitary "Egypt," the land is always referred to in its subdivided parts: *tꜣwy* (the two lands), *idbwy* (the two banks), *kmt* and *dšrt* (the black and red lands), and *šmꜥ* (Upper Egypt). Additionally, the third hymn of the cycle begins each line with "How great is the lord for his town," rather than for the whole of Egypt (Allen 2014, pp. 369–381). Some highly misleading translations of this text go so far as to imply that ancient Egypt had a concept similar to modern notions of citizenship, tying legal rights and protections to geographic sovereignty; for example, "How jubilant are your citizens, for you have fixed their boundaries" (Simpson 2003, p. 303 II.2). Yet the particular portion of the papyrus (UC 32157) where the word in question appears is heavily damaged, and other translations either omit a word here or have used terms like *msw* (children) instead (Allen 2014, p. 373 2.2). In fact, most of the Egyptian terms translated as "citizen" more accurately reflect the meaning of "townsperson" (Wb 1, 201.1), and no evidence exists to suggest that crossing borders was linked to a change in citizenship in ancient Egypt (Siegel 2022, p. 22).

Two of the most often cited examples of a unified "Egyptian" identity are both tied to cultural practice and geography. Both can be found in the Middle Kingdom Story of Sinuhe, and relate to hygiene and clothing, as well as the purported desire of all Egyptians to be buried in Egypt (Kemp 2006, p. 21; Matić 2020, p. 11). However, it is rarely acknowledged that both of these "universally Egyptian" episodes apply to only the highest elites. In the first example, Sinuhe returns to Egypt and sheds the vestiges of his life in West Asia. He is cleaned, groomed, and clad in white linen (Lichtheim 2006a, p. 233). Yet Sinuhe's transformation from ꜥꜣm (West Asian) back to "Egyptian" does not happen when he crosses some defined state border, but when he returns to the royal residence – he is also a high official with personal access to the royal family. Therefore, these customs of dress and hygiene are more likely to be representative of royal or high elite traditions, rather than representing some pan-Egyptian ethnicity (Candelora 2022b, p. 244). Even among this contemporary elite class, variation on adornment practices can be found within idealized settings; Middle Kingdom officials, especially in Middle Egypt, often depicted themselves in their tombs wearing brightly colored and intricately patterned textiles, presumably made of wool, rather than the expected white linen (Galczynski 2024, pp. 81–88; Moreno García 2024, p. 15).

Yet the urgent desire to be buried in Egypt is most often referenced as a symbol of a unified Egyptian identity. This supposedly "Egyptian" desire was recorded not only in Sinuhe but also in the autobiographies of Sabni and Pepinakht Heqaib, in which the bodies of deceased expeditionary officials were returned to Egypt for burial (Matić 2020, p. 11; Sethe 1932, Urk, I, 134, 13–17). Yet in these cases as well, it is only the highest of elites who might be able to afford such corporeal retrieval or be gifted it by the king. In the Shipwrecked Sailor, the serpent assures the sailor that he will die in his town, and Simpson even footnotes this line with an explanation that "burial in a foreign land was abhorrent to the Egyptians" (Simpson 2003, p. 50n7). Yet in this example, it is not Egypt in which the sailor wants to be buried, but in his hometown, presumably in the same necropolis where his family is buried. Additionally, most of these examples date to the Old or Middle Kingdoms, suggesting there may have been changes in this practice over time. In fact, there are several examples of New Kingdom Egyptian officials buried below the First Cataract in Nubia, and in the story of Wenamun, reference is made to Egyptians buried in the Levant (Buzon & Simonetti 2013; Di Biase-Dyson 2013, p. 336; Goelet 1999, p. 26). P. Insinger provides a Greco-Roman perspective on this issue, implying that the concern does not have to do with being buried away from Egypt, but being buried at all: "The one who dies away from his town, he gets buried only by pity" (P. Insinger 28, 7, Ragazzoli 2011, p. 29). This corresponds closely to pharaonic punishments for crimes considered especially heinous, in which the convicted would be executed and denied a proper burial, thus losing their access to an afterlife (Lorton 1977, pp. 17–23).

Other aspects that have been presented as stereotypical of "Egyptian-ness" are a common language, belief in a divine king, and a shared religion (Kemp 2006, p. 20; Matić 2020, pp. 10–11). While there was a common language, it exhibited regionalism and likely included at least five distinct dialects (Allen 2010; Hagen 2007, p. 250). In P. Anastasi I, one scribe complains the other is incomprehensible; "Your discourses ... are so confused when heard that no interpreter can unravel them. They are like a Delta man's conversation with a man of Elephantine" (Wente 1990, p. 109 letter 129). This satirical jab between scribes emphasizes the existence and extremity of these dialects, suggesting that individuals from the northern and southern areas of Egypt would have had difficulty communicating at all. This regionalism is also apparent in religion, for although the general pantheon was the same across Egypt, individual cities and regions focused their worship on particular deities or triads, as well as having their own creation myths (Dunand & Zivie-Coche 2005, pp. 25–28).

Another common "illusion égyptologique" is that Egypt was either isolated or isolationist (Zivie-Coche 2018, p. 24). This misconception is based on xenophobic, anti-foreigner rhetoric common in royal or literary texts, stemming from the duality of *ma'at* and *isfet*. This worldview, simplistically put, equates Egypt and Egyptians with cosmic order, *ma'at*, and foreigners and their lands with chaos (Assmann 2003, pp. 151–153; Chantrain 2019; Haring 2005, p. 164; Kemp 2006, pp. 22–23; Langer 2018; Langer & Fernández-Götz 2020, pp. 39–41; Loprieno 1988; Moers 2015; Schneider 2010, pp. 145–147; Taterka 2024, pp. 119–122). Archetypal scenes of kings upholding *ma'at* feature him smiting, sitting enthroned upon (Figure 8), or trampling bound foreigners (S.T. Smith 2007, pp. 223–229; Peirce 2019; Taterka 2024, p. 119). Certainly, border security and the prevention of foreign immigration was equated with *ma'at*, and the "influx of foreigners is one of the major motifs that define catastrophe and social disorder in 'pessimistic' literature" (Eyre 1990, p. 140). When viewed in tandem with the archaeological, textual, and artistic evidence for border forts and surveillance programs, one is left with an impression of an Egypt with closed borders that prevented mobility and/or migration (Moreno García 2024, pp. 5–10; Morris 2017; S.T. Smith 2005, pp. 210–215).

The Year 8 Semna Stele of Senwosret III (Figure 9 – Berlin 14753), erected at one of these border forts, is often cited as the prime example of the Egyptian

Figure 8 Bound foreigners beneath the thrones of Amenhotep III and Queen Tiye, tomb of Anen, Thebes – by Norman de Garis Davies, courtesy of the Metropolitan Museum of Art, CC0 1.0.

state claiming ownership of property, marked by a rigid border that prevented population movement (Vogel 2011, p. 322):

> (1) Southern border (*tꜣš*), which was made in year 8 under the majesty of the double king Chakaure [Senwosret III], given life for ever (2) and ever, not to allow, that it will passed by any Nubian travelling to the north, (3) travelling on land or by a Nubian ship, and also any cattle of (4) a Nubian, except a Nubian, who comes to merchandize in Iqen (Mirgissa), (5) with a message or anything, which can be done well together with him. It will not be allowed, (6) that an indigenous ship of a Nubian will pass Heh by sailing northwards in eternity! (translation after Kootz 2013, p. 46)

However, the only caveat preventing Nubians crossing the border was that they stop at the fortress of Mirgissa to declare themselves and what they may have to trade – in this case, they were welcome to pass. Siegel notes that border transgressions were generally painted as "a personal affront to the pharaoh's power" rather than a failure of the border (Siegel 2022, p. 20). Despite this edict, archaeological evidence from southern Egypt suggests that Nubians were able to cross and settle in Egyptian territory for millennia (Adams 1984; de Souza 2019; Hafsaas-Tsakos 2010; Irish & Friedman 2010; Knoblauch 2019; Liszka 2015, 2022; Schneider 2010; Smither 1945). Thus the issue does not seem to have been immigration or border crossing in general, but rather unsanctioned

Figure 9 Small Semna Stele of Senwosret III (Berlin 14753) – by author after Meurer 1996, T. 1.

cases of foreigners settling in Egypt without the knowledge of the state. This state oversight of immigration likely applied to the *wnt* and *sgr* settlement types, as well as the late New Kingdom resettlement of Libyans and Sea Peoples within Egypt, probably ensuring they were incorporated into tax-paying structures (Moreno García 2024, pp. 12–13; Siegel 2022, p. 20).

Certainly, the rhetorical topos proclaims a stark contrast between Egyptian and foreign, "seeing the world in black and white" (Langer 2018, p. 50). However, in practice, the *ma'at/isfet*, Egyptian/foreigner dichotomy was not at all rigid. These opposites instead reflected different ends of a spectrum rather than an either/or. Both pairs were mutually constituted, in that both were required for the other to exist meaningfully and be recognizable; there would be no order without chaos, and no self without the other. Additionally, context dictated where someone might fall along the spectrum, a fluidity that can be found throughout the Egyptian worldview. Seth was the literal embodiment of chaos, a negative force, until his chaos was needed to aid in Re's journey. Hathor and Sakhmet are also excellent divine examples of this spectrum, as they were often considered the ordered and chaotic forms of the same divinity. In many cases, Egyptians were manifestations of *isfet* rather than *ma'at*; Upper and Lower Egypt could be included as part of the Nine Bows, and Egyptians were named among the enemy leaders in the Execration Texts (Muhlestein 2008; Uphill 1967, pp. 394–395). Conversely, foreigners could also be representative of *ma'at* by serving the king, especially on campaign. This is illustrated, for example, in the orderly rows of Sherden marching for Ramses II in his various Qadesh reliefs (Figure 10) (Abbas 2017).

Individuals from Egypt could and did assume foreign identities, as exemplified by Sinuhe making a life for himself in West Asia. Upon his return to Egypt, the king said, "Look, Sinuhe has returned as an Asian that the Asiatics have created" (Allen 2010, p. 142). In P. Anastasi I, while a hapless scribe is abroad, his groom flees in the night; "He consorts with the Shasu Beduin tribes and assumes the guise of an Asiatic" (Wente 1990, p. 107). Both Egyptians and foreigners were considered *rmṯ*, people, and were capable of losing their humanity (Chantrain 2019; Moers 2005). In all, it seems that the conception

Figure 10 Relief of Sherden marching for Ramses II at the Battle of Qadesh, Abydos – by author.

of what it meant to be Egyptian or foreign was less a clear-cut, rigid dichotomy based on borders, geographic origin, or cosmic worldview, but rather a fluid understanding that could shift based on context.

3.3 Regional Identities

For most of human history, and arguably still today, local and regional identities superseded many others, especially the sense of belonging to a nation or empire. Regional identity characterizes groups that both subdivide and cross the border of the state, essentially those that do not fit the homogenizing, dominant identity discourse (Paasi 2003). For instance, in early twentieth-century Italy, individuals were far more likely to ascribe to identities linked to extended families, villages, or regions, than to consider themselves "Italian." In fact, differences between northern and southern Italians were extreme enough that spoken dialects impeded communication and cultural differences, which aligned more with European or Mediterranean groups respectively, and inspired mutual disdain. Individuals did not identify as collectively Italian until they immigrated to foreign countries, though even these diasporic groups tended to cluster by home region (Gabaccia 1999). In much of the premodern world, these regional identities were tied to kinship networks and their long association with a "hometown" (Langer & Fernández-Götz 2020, p. 37; Terlouw 2009).

The same tie to hometowns can be seen throughout Egyptian history, especially in autobiographical and didactic texts. Moers argues that "hometown and region are the key factor of social attribution" in Egypt, starting at least in the Old Kingdom and evident most clearly in the intermediate periods (Moers 2015, p. 696). Perhaps the most paradigmatic examples come from First Intermediate Period autobiographies; Iti of Gebelein proclaimed, "I am an excellent townsman who acts with his strength. I am an important pillar in the Theban region and a role-model in the south" (Figure 11) (CG 20001 1 l. 2–4, Landgráfová 2011, pp. 68–70). The roughly contemporary autobiography of Mereri declared that he was "a loved one of the whole city of Dendara, a praised one of his town" (Schenkel 1965, p. 130). Similar sentiments can be found through the Late Period, including on the block statue of Harwa from the Twenty-Fifth Dynasty (Berlin 8163, Moers 2015, p. 696). Wisdom literature from the Middle Kingdom through the Greco-Roman period, including the Teachings of Ptahhotep, Ani, Amenemope, Ankhshesonqi, and pIsinger, continuously emphasize the importance of family, being known and liked in your town, as well as being wary of outsiders (Hagen 2007, pp. 244–248; Moers 2015, pp. 696–698).

In Egypt, outsiders or strangers need not be foreigners, but simply individuals who are unknown to one's townspeople; in the Teaching of Ani, young men are

Figure 11 Stele of Iti and Neferu, Suppl. 13114 – courtesy of the Mueso Egizio. CC0 1.0.

warned to "beware of a woman who is a stranger, one not known in her town" (Lichtheim 2006b, p. 137). The ancient Egyptian concept of self-identity "may look entirely different abroad, which, in Egypt, might begin very close to home" (Moers 2015, p. 698). Indeed, individuals traveling to different regions would encounter different dialects, landscapes, climates, and peoples. The word most often used to describe entering *kmt*, *hȝj* (descend), could also be applied to people leaving their home regions starting in the Old Kingdom (Candelora 2022b, p. 242; Moers 2015, pp. 695–696; Parkinson 2012, p. 26). Interestingly, the same root was used in a Third Intermediate Period text to emphasize an individual's sense of belonging. The inscription states, "I belong (*n.j wj*) to Thebes, I have been born in her, I am not a non-local (*hȝj*)" (Louvre C 258 l. 5, Moers 2015, p. 696). The disturbance and feelings of unbelonging that even intra-Egyptian travel could cause was also mentioned in the Story of Sinuhe. Describing his disorientation at finding himself in West Asia, Sinuhe finds the most relatable parallel to be "like a Deltan seeing himself in Elephantine" (Allen 2014, p. 79), indicating not just the geographic but also the cultural dislocation one might experience in a distant region of Egypt. New Kingdom writings known as "praises of cities" express "homesick alienation" and poetic longing for one's hometown, clarifying that officials viewed being away on missions as equivalent to exile (Moers 2010, p. 695; also see Lichtheim 1980; Ragazzoli 2011, p. 27). It is apparent that local or regional identity was of far more significance to the ancient Egyptians than any sense of supposed "national" belonging (Assmann 1996, p. 97; Candelora 2022b, pp. 244–248; Hagen 2007; Matić 2020, pp. 11–12; Moers 2015; Schneider 2010, p. 145).

4 Borderlands and Immigration

The prioritization of regional identity, as well as the vague and permeable "state" borders discussed in Sections 2 and 3, suggests that ancient Egyptians experienced a "multiplicity of borders, which may operate on different levels at different times" (Mullin 2011b, p. 103). Similarly, Parker argued that the Assyrian imperial frontier in Anatolian was comprised of multidimensional and overlapping boundaries, consisting of geographic, political, demographic, cultural, and economic divisions (Parker 2006), while Green and Costion developed the Cross-Cultural Interaction Model to visually represent the complexity of such frontier interfaces (Green & Costion 2017). Borders are not only locations and political demarcations but also social phenomena and institutions; bordering practices actively draw and maintain boundaries between groups that are largely defined through interaction with an "other." Such boundaries differentiate, but also allow for crossing over, serving as meeting points and zones of interaction (Baud & Van Schendel 1997, p. 216). This approach reframes borders as borderlands, places where identities are created, intersect, and are transformed (Anzaldúa 1987; Lightfoot & Martinez 1995; Mullin 2011a). Borderland identity is a highly local, flexible commodity that can be situational, strategic, and transient (Hämäläinen & Truett, 2011, p. 348; Lightfoot, 2008; Lightfoot & Martinez, 1995).

Instances of cultural interaction can be approached via a broad collection of postcolonial theories (Candelora 2022a). The study of ethnicity is relevant to the examination of immigration as human mobility tends to bring different ethnic groups into contact, and it is the comparison itself that helps define the groups. Similarly to broader identity theories, ethnicity theories define social groups as constructed collectives that are ascribed to by the individual and affirmed by those both within and beyond the group, and also see ethnicity as flexible and context-dependent (Barth 1969; Bentley 1987; Emberling 1997; Jones 1997; Lucy 2005; Matić 2020; Shennan 1989; Smith 2003). In applying these concepts to ancient interactions, many viewed material culture to be a direct expression of identity. However, this requires identity or ethnic groups to be firmly bounded, which they are not; instead, "material culture represents numerous relationships between people and things, as well as between things, and thus networks" (Bader 2021, p. 21). Such "complex webs of economic, political, social and cultural linkages" between material and people have been the focus of theories of entanglement that work to understand what exactly material culture reveals about the humans who produced and used it (Dietler 2010, p. 53; Hodder 2012; Stockhammer 2012a).

Several studies provide excellent discussions of the history and difficulties inherent in studying migration via material culture, both in Egypt and elsewhere in the ancient world (Bader 2012, 2021, pp. 15–40; de Souza 2020; Knapp 2008, pp. 30–65, 2021, pp. 2–9; Lightfoot 2008; Liszka 2012, pp. 41–132; Mourad 2021, pp. 25–44; Priglinger 2018). Frameworks drawn from biology and linguistics, such as hybridity, creolization, and mestizaje, have been used to characterize the blended nature of material culture that results from cross-cultural or interethnic interaction. Although helpful for understanding the finished artifacts as reflections of that contact, these theories tend to be more descriptive than explanatory. Bader stresses that reasonable interpretations of "ethnic markers" from the archaeological record, especially pottery, must take into account "the complete context and the several types of evidence of these finds and the way they are used" (Bader 2021, p. 31). This holistic picture centers more on the way material culture was fashioned and utilized, as well as how individuals received that socialized knowledge, acknowledging that identity is not embodied in the finished product, but in the constellation of practices surrounding it (Bourdieu 1977; Lave & Wenger 1991; Lightfoot *et al.* 1998; Maran & Stockhammer 2012; Stockhammer 2012b; Wendrich 2012; Wenger 1998).

The contact zones themselves, whether real or imagined spaces, have been theorized as particularly flexible, liminal areas wherein distinct identities meet, clash, blend, and transform. This has been theorized as Bhabha's "Third Space," Kopytoff's "ecumene," and White's "Middle Ground," but each concept notes that these zones are characterized by entanglement and exchange because the groups in contact are attempting to understand and accommodate one another. This process results in novel cultural production, hybridized material culture, mutually constituted worldviews, and practices that draw selectively on both traditions to form altogether new customs and identities (Bhabha 1994; Kopytoff 1987, p. 10; White 1991, 2006).

Borderlands are precisely these types of spaces, perhaps with the additional quality that their very liminality allows for even more cultural flexibility (Anzaldúa 1987; Hämäläinen & Truett 2011). Anzaldúa described the United States–Mexico borderland as the locus where "two worlds [merge] to form a third country – a border culture" (Anzaldúa 1987, p. 3). Within these regions, daily face-to-face interactions between distinct identity groups allow people to accommodate one another, including transforming their material and nonmaterial traditions (Baud & Van Schendel 1997, p. 216; Feuer 2016, p. 12).

As many have noted before, potentially ethnic identifying terms such as "Egyptian," "West Asian," "Nubian," "Libyan," etcetera, are both convenient and difficult to change; this type of generalization "allows dialogue to occur" while obscuring natural diversity (Bader 2021, p. 11n24; Kemp 2018, p. vi). Therefore, I follow Bader in clarifying that the use of these terms is not meant to ascribe an ethnic identity to either the culture or people discussed here, but rather to identify the broad geographical region in which the most parallels are found (Bader 2021, p. 72).

4.1 Immigrants in Ancient Egypt

Early studies of immigration approached cultural interaction and transformation via assimilation models. Assimilation presupposes several things about the cultural encounter: that the exchange is unidirectional, that the host society is superior to that of the immigrant, that the immigrant benefits from "unlearning" their original culture, and that ethnic or immigrant communities such as enclaves act only as temporary waystations en route to full assimilation and integration into the host society (Alba & Nee 1997, 2003). In the case of immigration in ancient Egypt, the same assumptions are engrained in the concept of Egyptianization, namely that any immigrants would have sought to assimilate, as completely as possible, to the "superior" Egyptian culture. For instance, a common refrain is: "Egyptianized foreigners had the ability to be assimilated into Egyptian society and the adoption of local religious and burial practices, behaviors, language, and material culture would see the disappearance of indicators of a non-Egyptian presence" (Hubschmann 2010a, p. 185; discussing O'Connor 2003, p. 159; Kitchen 1990, p. 21; for refutation of this idea, see Candelora 2019a, 2022a; Cohen 1992; de Souza 2013; Leahy 1985; Moreno García & Schneider 2018; Schneider 2006; Smith 2003; Van Pelt 2013). Much of this conceptualization has been predicated on the cosmological view of the foreigner as a manifestation of chaos (see Section 3.2), which by default categorizes them as a barbaric antagonist and prevents their acceptance and incorporation into Egyptian society. For instance, Langer argues: "Recalling that foreigners were part of Izfet by default it appears highly unlikely that they could be transformed into quasi-Egyptians" (Langer 2018, p. 65). From the perspective of Egyptian ideology, it can be difficult to imagine a situation in which an immigrant could become Egyptian; even the use of "quasi" emphasizes two crucial assumptions – that there was a unified, normative way to be Egyptian, and that foreigners would always fail to fully achieve that form. Langer acknowledges that "In reality, of course, individual foreigners could well integrate into New Kingdom society, although it has to remain unclear to what extent foreigners could overall blend in with Egyptians or what the 'success rate' of integration was" (Langer 2018, p. 66). Yet the underlying impression is that immigrants' ultimate goal should be to assimilate completely to this "Egyptian" culture.

However, it has been demonstrated that a normative or national Egyptian identity did not exist, suggesting that immigrants were adapting to localized cultural norms that may not have been defined by their holders, or seen by us, as Egyptian. Further, the assimilation model does not account for any influence of the immigrant on the host society nor immigrants' continued maintenance of their identities of origin, even across multiple generations. Instead, new theoretical frameworks dealing with cultural interaction and immigration scenarios agree that exchange and influence is multidirectional, resulting in entirely new cultural and material production drawing from all traditions. Alba and Nee refer to this as "composite culture," which evolved "out of the interpenetration of diverse cultural practices and beliefs" (Alba & Nee 2003, p. 10). They acknowledge that mainstream culture is already "highly variegated," but that this new, composite culture consists of "multiple interpenetrating layers and allows individuals and subpopulations to forge identities out of its materials to distinguish themselves from others in the mainstream" (Alba & Nee 2003, p. 13).

Newer approaches account for a range of acculturative options that immigrants can choose to employ strategically in different contexts, which may be affected by other intersectional aspects of their identity such as social status or gender (Berry 1997; Dietler 1998, p. 299; Knapp 2008, p. 64; Phinney et al. 2001). This includes targeted assimilation, but also appropriation, adaptation, selective incorporation, indifference, or outright rejection of any aspect of culture, from belief to material (Dietler 2010). Indeed, psychological studies of modern immigrants have shown the highest mental health among those who employed a range of approaches, adapting elements from the host culture alongside the maintenance of traditions from their homelands (Phinney et al. 2001). Evidence from ancient Egypt demonstrates that immigrants applied many of these strategies in adapting to their new homes.

Despite the enduring illusion of ancient Egypt as isolated and xenophobic, interactions with foreigners and foreigners immigrating to and settling in Egypt occurred throughout pharaonic history. Immigrants would cease to be considered "foreign" if they lived in the Nile Valley, instead, as Schneider puts it, becoming Egyptians "of foreign origin" (Schneider 2010, p. 144; see also Assmann 1996, p. 97; Schneider 2003, 2006). Ethnonyms like ꜥꜣm or nḥsj were applied to foreigners abroad as well as to acculturated members of Egyptian society (Chantrain 2019; Priglinger 2019; Schneider 2010, p. 144), suggesting that their diverse ethnic origin was no impediment to their integration into pharaonic cultures. In his First Intermediate Period stela from Gebelein, Qedes, a soldier of Nubian descent, boasted, "I surpassed this whole town in swiftness, its Nubians and its Southerners" (Schenkel 1965, p. 61). This demonstrates that not only he, but other Nubians as well, were considered unproblematic members of the town of Gebelein (Moers 2015, p. 696). It is also interesting to note that Qedes defines the population of Gebelein as consisting specifically of Nubians and Southerners, rather than Egyptians, emphasizing the higher significance of regional identities. Several other groups of foreign mercenaries also relocated and were integrated into Egyptian society over the *longue durée* (Abbas 2017; Emanuel 2013; Schneider 2010, p. 147). In the Story of Wenamun, the protagonist declared that "those who sail under Smendes are Egyptian crews (*jst kmt*). He has no Syrian crews (*jst ḫr.w*)" (Lichtheim 2006b, p. 226), suggesting that individuals of foreign descent, regardless of where they were located in the world or what practices they followed, were considered Egyptians if they worked for the king. This ability of foreigners to become Egyptian is even reflected in Hittite texts. The Deeds of Šuppiluliuma I stated that the "Storm-god of Ḫattuša carried the man (collective singular) of Kuruštama, a Hittite subject, to the land of Egypt and made them Egyptians" (Vigo 2024, p. 122). This example implies, in this case from an etic perspective, that the only requirement for being Egyptian was living in the Nile Valley.

Schneider crucially noted that a simplistic application of the foreigner topos was not an accurate reflection of the Egyptian worldview, as the degree and nature of cultural interaction with foreigners changed over time (Schneider 2010, p. 147; Taterka 2024, p. 118). Relatively small-scale contact via trade, mobility, and military engagements characterized the Predynastic Period and the Old Kingdom. A smattering of evidence in the Old Kingdom suggests that foreigners relocated to Egypt, whether voluntarily or involuntarily as prisoners of war (Spalinger 1979). The autobiographies of Weni and Harkhuf record the use of Nubian mercenaries, and Nubians are also employed as attendants to high elites buried at Giza. *ꜥmw* (im)migrants appear on the Sahure and Unas pyramid causeways, showing seafaring sailors and emaciated groups (Schneider 2010, pp. 150–151). An increase in Nubian immigration, specifically to centers in the south like Gebelein, Hierakonpolis (HK27 C), and Aswan, is attested mainly in burial evidence from the First Intermediate Period (Irish & Friedman 2010; Meurer 1996).

Especially as contact and exchange with neighboring regions increased from the Middle Kingdom onward, Egypt was exposed to new groups of people and various sources presented more nuanced, context-dependent perceptions of foreigners and immigrants. The Middle Kingdom and Second Intermediate Period saw an influx of foreigners recorded in textual and archaeological evidence. Immigrants who retained foreign names, sometimes alongside assigned Egyptian names (P. Brooklyn 35.1446), occupied almost 100 different professions spanning all social classes, and in funerary contexts these immigrant families sometimes maintained their foreign naming traditions for generations (Mourad 2013; Saretta 2016; Schneider 2003). Middle Egyptian tombs and inscriptions record the presence of Nubian, Southwest Asian, Libyan, and Eastern Desert soldiers in officials' militias (Figure 12) (Moreno García 2024, pp. 10–17; Newberry 1893). Archaeological evidence from the Eastern Delta indicates immigration from West Asia (Bader 2011; Bietak 2010; Mourad 2015, 2021; Priglinger 2019; Redmount 1995; Stantis & Schutkowski 2019). Medjay individuals worked for the Egyptian crown (Liszka 2012), while cemetery and ceramic data from the valley preserve our only testimony of Pan-Grave immigration (de Souza 2013, 2019; Meurer 1996; Schneider 2003).

By the New Kingdom, the evidence for immigration increased, and the acceptance, display, and even celebration of diversity was heightened in this period. In the Eighteenth Dynasty, some of the highest offices of state were occupied by individuals who were born outside of Egypt, such as Thutmose III's Mitannian wives (Lilyquist 2003); by people with foreign names like Aper-El, the vizier under Amenhotep III/Akhenaten (Zivie 2014); or by people who may have been of foreign descent such as Maiherpri, who was given the high honor of a burial in the Valley of the Kings (Lakomy 2016; see also discussions and caveats in Matić 2020, p. 13; Schneider 2010, p. 155; Taterka 2024, pp. 127–128). This expanding acceptance was also made clear in religious texts. The

Figure 12 Foreigners, east wall of the chapel of Khnumhotep I (No. 14), Beni Hasan – by author after Newberry 1893: pl. 47.

hymns to Amun-Re (P. Bulaq 17) and the Great Hymn to the Aten acknowledged that these gods created all peoples, including foreigners, and did not imply their subordination to Egyptians, while in the fourth hour of the Book of Gates, foreigners were able to participate in the afterlife. Foreign names were preserved more often by the New Kingdom, and increasing attention was paid to the nuanced artistic rendering of difference in cultural costumes (Haring 2005; Schneider 2010, p. 154). The impact of immigrants can be seen across Egyptian society in the importation and adaptation of new technologies, foreign loan words, literary and artistic motifs, religion, and more (Candelora 2019a, 2020, 2023; Cornelius 1994, 2004; Hoch 1994; Mourad 2019, 2021; Schneider 2006, 2008, 2011; Winand 2017).

By the first millennium BCE, foreigners and immigration were central to the characterization of Egypt. Many more Libyans as well as new groups, including Judeans, Phoenicians, Carians, and Ionians, settled in Egypt and often served as mercenaries. Naukratis was founded to serve as the main Greek trading port, and became home to sailors from all over the Eastern Mediterranean world (Hasdemir Bozkuş 2023). This period also saw a series of foreign reigns, including Libyan, Napatan, Assyrian, Persian, and Ptolemaic, which affected immigration, cultural expression, and identity (Jansen-Winkeln 2000; Johnson 1999; Mathieson *et al.* 1995; Schneider 2010, pp. 155–156; Taterka 2024, pp. 130–133). As is evident from this brief survey, immigration was a constant reality throughout Egyptian history, only increasing over the *longue durée*, while the reception of immigrants was constantly transforming based on context.

4.2 Immigrant Identities

It should be stressed that in the millennia of immigration to Egypt, full Egyptianization was never the only acculturative outcome to be pursued. In each case, immigrants struck an "acculturative balance" between their cultures of origin and their new host society (Berry 1997, p. 9; Phinney *et al.* 2001, p. 495), often producing hybrid material culture and new identities. Indeed, modern immigrants often commodify their "ethnic capital," advertising their foreignness or "deliberately cultivat[ing] specific ethnic markers" to improve their lives (Kim 2019, p. 358). This capitalization allows immigrants to alter relationships of power with locals, positioning themselves as the expert in certain skills or products linked with their ethnicity, and earning them credit in both economic and social form (Kim 2019; Li 2004).

Numerous examples of such capitalization can be found among immigrants in ancient Egypt, especially in particular craft traditions and among mercenary groups. Textual records preserve examples of textile producers, vintners, and boatbuilders who not only maintained West Asian naming practices, often over generations (which in and of itself is not a marker of foreignness), but were also sought after for their expertise, which was conceived of as West Asian (Candelora 2019a, pp. 30–34; Galczynski 2024, pp. 227–233, 241–245; Morris 2014, p. 371). Specifically Nubian and Eastern Desert mercenary groups were recorded as serving the Egyptian king and officials by the late Old Kingdom, and evidence for the immigration of some of these groups appears not long after (Liszka 2012; Meurer 1996). These people likely brought new leatherworking techniques and emphasized their Nubian identities in pursuing careers as hunters, herders, entertainers, and more (Moreno García 2024, pp. 9, 14). By the New Kingdom, foreign mercenaries were also drawn from West Asia, especially those who were considered *maryannu*, charioteers (Gnirs 1996; Moorey 2001), and at least some of these immigrants capitalized on their foreignness as a sign of their chariotry skill. One example is Berlin Stele ÄM 14122 from Amarna, depicting a man utilizing common Egyptian artistic motifs to denote West Asian origins, including a particular hairstyle and large beard (Figure 13). He also bears a likely semitic name, Trr,

Figure 13 Stele of a Syrian soldier drinking, ÄM 14122 – Staatliche Museen zu Berlin, Ägyptisches Museum und Papyrussammlung / Sandra Steiß CC BY-SA 4.0.

and has a spear behind him, a weapon associated with charioteers. His wife, who is shown in a more stereotypically Egyptian style aside from her red skin tone, also has a non-Egyptian name (Haring 2005, pp. 168–169; Schneider 1992, pp. 237–238). In this case, it is likely the elite Trr commissioned the stela, suggesting that he was intentionally highlighting ethnic markers that would associate him with a West Asian tradition of skilled charioteers (Candelora 2019a, pp. 32–34).

Even the foreigners who ruled Egypt (many of whom lived there and thus should be considered immigrants) capitalized on or at least preserved aspects of their foreign identities. The Hyksos, the Libyan rulers of the Third Intermediate Period, the Napatans, and the Persians all kept their original personal names, adopting titles and throne names from the Egyptian repertoire. The Libyans even brought culturally specific titles such as Chief of the Ma, Libu, or Meshwesh while the Hyksos adopted an Egyptian title for themselves (ḥḳꜣ ḫꜣswt, rulers of foreign lands), potentially to highlight their foreignness (Candelora 2017; Leahy 1985). These immigrant rulers also brought and adapted elements of their native styles of rule to Egypt. The Hyksos seem to have retained a kinship-based governmental structure with broad powers and a style of diplomacy common in contemporary West Asia (Candelora 2019a). The Libyans operated using a more feudally based arrangement that may have reflected their native tribal organization (Broekman 2010; Cole 2015; Jansen-Winkeln 1999). The Twenty-Fifth Dynasty conversely took a more contextualized approach to state control, accepting vassalage in the Delta but exerting more direct influence in the south, and incorporating royal women into the ruling structure (Lohwasser 2001; Pope 2014; Török 2008, pp. 311–376). The Napatan kings also showed themselves as distinct from the standard Egyptian monarch through visual markers such as the skull cap, double uraeus, and ram's-head necklace (Russmann 1995, p. 232). In the Libyan Period, it seems to have been primarily the elite, rather than the kings themselves, who continued to be shown wearing potential identity markers like feathers, either vertically or horizontally, on their heads (Cooney 2011, pp. 279–291). Additionally, the only six extant examples of falcon-headed coffins or cartonnages all belong to elites or kings of the Libyan Period, perhaps indicating a visual display of distinct identities (Broekman 2009). Also in the Persian Period, many elite and royal depictions, such as the statue of Udjahorresnet, Ptahhotep, or the Suez stelae of Darius, elected to adopt, maintain, or evoke elements like the Achaemenid court robe and lion-headed bracelets (Colburn 2020; Cooney 1954; Lloyd 2007). The continued use of potentially foreign visual markers certainly linked elites with the current regime, and in the case of the rulers themselves may have served to remind their Egyptian subjects not only of their origins but also of their ties to power brokers and trade networks abroad.

Furthermore, identity markers were maintained for presumably more personal reasons of ascription rather than capitalization. West Asian immigrants may have preserved personal adornment traditions through dress and toggle pins (Figure 14) (Bader 2021, p. 30, but see important caveats on p. 92), as well as weaponry and burial customs (Bader 2011, 2021, pp. 52–54, again with significant cautions; Forstner-Müller 2008, 2010; Philip 2006). For the various Libyan groups in Egypt, the conservation of their western identities included Libyan personal names, forms of social structure, the use of feather adornment, and burial practices (Broekman 2010; Broekman *et al.* 2009; Cole 2015; Jansen-Winkeln 1999; Leahy 1985; Naunton 2010; O'Connor 1987). Examples from the Persian Period can also be found in the continued use of ethnic identifiers, shows of group solidarity, and religious traditions among the various groups living at Elephantine (Becking 2022).

Another particularly interesting example is the funerary stele of Djedherbes from Saqqara (Figure 15). The stele displays a funerary inscription in both the hieroglyphic and Demotic scripts, and lists Djedherbes's mother as Tanofrether and father as Artam, clearly Egyptian and Persian names respectively. The lunette features a winged sun disc that, due to the addition of a feathered tail

Figure 14 Southwest Asians from the tomb of Khnumhotep II (Tomb 3), Beni Hassan – By Norman de Garis Davies, courtesy of the Metropolitan Museum of Art, CC0 1.0.

Figure 15 Stele of Djedherbes, Saqqara – by author after Mathieson *et al.* 1995, figure 3.

and spirals in place of pendent uraei, bears more resemblance to Achaemenid symbols of Zoroastrianism than the typical Egyptian version. Further, while the upper register is a relatively standard scene of the deceased being mummified by Anubis, the lower register selectively combines elements from an Egyptian offering scene and an Achaemenid presentation scene (Mathieson *et al.* 1995). Interestingly, in the inscriptions Djedherbes did not claim either Egyptian or Persian identities, but the collective may suggest his embodiment of a third identity characteristic of this southwestern borderland of the Persian Empire. This fascinating find also emphasizes the need to develop new frameworks to better understand not just immigration in ancient Egypt, but also second-generation and later descendants.

5 Borderland Identities

The goal of the following case studies is to demonstrate the entanglement of borders and immigration, as well as the potential of borderlands theory to reframe our approaches to the ontological relationship between these concepts. In the study of ancient Egypt, liminal places and their populations are often approached differently if that place is viewed as part of a sovereign territory called Egypt. Research questions concerning foreigners are developed around the existence of a national, pan-Egyptian identity, contained within geopolitical borders, to compare them against. By recentering the border, regardless of whether it falls between Egypt and foreign lands or within Egypt itself, it is possible to focus instead on local identity expressions, working from the bottom up to investigate human agency, accommodation, and adaptation in the negotiation of interactions between different groups. Further, while traditional approaches to borders necessitate rigid distinctions between primordial identities (Jones 1997), a borderlands framework presupposes that the interacting identities are inherently fluid and constantly changing.

Knapp has noted the "multiplicity of problems involved in *defining*" an identity and has suggested that archaeologists focus on the ways in which that identity was constructed (Knapp 2008, p. 63) – here understood as the bordering processes involved, and how that identity was communicated to or performed for society. These case studies are not meant to be exhaustive treatments of borders and hybridity or entanglement along Egypt's edges, as each has been examined much more thoroughly in the sources cited. My aim is to reconsider these cases from a borderlands perspective to investigate how immigration and adaptation operate multidirectionally within these liminal spaces, allowing for a more nuanced perception of both borders (or lack thereof) and the identities specific to these zones.

5.1 The Nile Cataracts

This region, including Egypt's southern expanse as well as Lower Nubia, has the most developed scholarly tradition of investigation into borders and identity (to name just a few: Adams 1984; Cohen 1992; de Souza 2019; Liszka 2012; Minor 2012; Smith 2003; Smith & Buzon 2018; Török 2008; Zibelius-Chen 1988). I hesitate to refer to this region as the Egypto–Nubian border, as even this terminology inherently assumes primordially distinct identities defined by a geopolitical border. This borderland spanned from somewhere north of the First Cataract to around the Third Cataract, and is actually defined by a lack of firm border, which moved depending on context – including both chronological and social contexts, as well as ideological versus administrative perspectives.

For instance, in the Middle Kingdom, Lower Nubia was included in the administration of the "Head of the South" along with Upper Egypt forming a border at Cusae, while the contemporary politico-ideological border is usually considered to have been located at the Second Cataract (Smith 1997, p. 82, 2005a). Various trajectories of immigration have been demonstrated within this borderland; C-Group and Eastern Desert immigrants (if we should even class them as immigrants at all, as opposed to natives to this broad borderland) settled in Upper Egypt (see Section 4.1; de Souza 2019; Hafsaas-Tsakos 2010; Irish & Friedman 2010; Liszka 2012). People from cities like Thebes also immigrated south, settling at sites like Tombos, and "Egyptian" soldiers were stationed in the fortresses at the Second Cataract (Buzon *et al.* 2007; Buzon & Bowen 2010; Buzon & Simonetti 2013; Smith 1995, 2003, 2013; Smith & Buzon 2018). The following case study examines the personal responses of immigrants as borders shifted around them.

In the late Middle Kingdom or Second Intermediate Period, Egyptian state control of Lower Nubia waned. The soldiers stationed in these fortresses had been living alongside and/or interacting commonly with various local groups, including Kermans and C-Group Nubians for decades in this borderland. Stuart T. Smith has been able to convincingly demonstrate the intensifying mixture of these communities through the Second Intermediate Period, when the state-claimed, politico-ideological border presumably shifted back from Semna to the region of Elephantine (Smith 1991, 1995). Stelae from the fortress of Buhen, dating to this period of heightened entanglement, reveal interesting autobiographical information about two men who likely identified primarily as culturally Egyptian – whether they were born in Egypt or to "Egyptian" families stationed at the fortress.

The stelae of Sepedher, the commandant of Buhen (Figure 16), and Ka, an official (Figure 17), are both from the stylistic, linguistic, titulary, and religious traditions common to Egypt. They are round-topped stelae with winged sun discs and wadjet eyes in the lunettes respectively, as well as *ḥtp-di-nsw* offering formulae written in (if somewhat difficult) Middle Egyptian hieroglyphs. All of the family members of Ka and Sepedher, known from these stelae and another erected by Sepedher in honor of his brother (Philadelphia 10983), have Egyptian personal names (Säve-Söderbergh 1949, p. 55) – again, not alone strong indicators of identity, but taken in tandem with all the other Egyptian elements, may suggest a potential expression of group belonging.

These stelae are remarkable in that they both refer to these individuals serving not an Egyptian king, but the ruler of Kush. Sepedher proclaimed, "I was a valiant commandant of Buhen, and never did any commandant do what I did; I built the temple of Horus, Lord of Buhen, to the satisfaction of the

Figure 16 Stele of Sepedher (Philadelphia 10984), Buhen – by author after Säve-Söderbergh 1949, figure 1.

ruler of Cush" (translation after Säve-Söderbergh 1949, p. 55). Such claims of supremacy and uniqueness are typical of Egyptian autobiographical stelae, as is the task of constructing, embellishing, or refurbishing religious installations to the satisfaction of the king. Ka says outright, "I was a valiant servant of the ruler of Cush; I washed [my] feet in the waters of Cush in the suite of the ruler *Nḏḥ*, and I returned safe and sound [to my] family" (translation after Säve-Söderbergh 1949, p. 52). The first statement is a bald declaration that he served the Kerman king, and Säve-Söderbergh interpreted the difficult and unparalleled feet-washing passage as a ceremonial expression of loyalty (Säve-Söderbergh 1949, p. 53). Finally, Ka returned home to Buhen, not Egypt, to his family, which included not just his children, but eventually at least his grandchildren as well, as Ka's grandson, Ahwoser, was the dedicator of the stele.

Immigration and Borders in Ancient Egypt 49

Figure 17 Stele of Ka (Khartoum 18), Buhen – by author after Säve-Söderbergh 1949, figure 2.

Consequently, these two individuals are intriguing examples of identity negotiation in borderland contexts. Ka at least is a member of a multigenerational family belonging to that borderland, and both he and Sepedher reveal devotion to a local borderland deity, Horus of Buhen. Their stelae served as public monuments that allowed for expressions or advertisement of their identities and group ascriptions, at least to the community in the region of Buhen who were able to read or interpret them. Publicly then, both men expressed a majority of elements that align most closely with Egyptian traditions, while proudly declaring that they served the ruler of Kush – a statement that would set them against not just Egyptian political alignment but also the *ma'at/isfet* worldview. It would seem that as the political border shifted around Buhen, the community centered there did not express a profound shift in identity. Whether the border moved during the lifetimes of Ka and Sepedher, or that of their ancestors, these men were apparently unperturbed by changing political allegiances, and seem to have belonged first and foremost to the borderland and its local traditions and exigencies.

5.2 The Eastern Desert

The Eastern Desert is a vast region spanning from the Mediterranean coast in the north to well into modern Sudan and Eritrea. In the ancient world, this zone was home to various nomadic or seminomadic groups, who often interacted with the inhabitants of the Nile Valley, whether expeditions for trade and raw materials traversed the desert, or because the nomads found temporary work or settled in the valley permanently (Barnard & Duistermaat 2012; Barnard & Wendrich 2008; Darnell 2021; Förster & Riemer 2013; Liszka 2012). It is a borderland region whose many toponyms reflect the diversity of groups living within it, including not only groups categorized broadly as Nubian, such as the Medjay and Pan-Grave, but also ꜥꜣmw and more (Barnard 2013; Cooper 2015; Tallet 2009). The next case study was selected because it has often been discussed as an example of immigrant acculturation so complete that they "disappeared" from the archaeological record (see excellent discussion in de Souza 2013).

The Pan-Grave Culture has been identified through archaeological evidence, mainly in the form of characteristic burials, at sites in the Nile Valley from Lower Nubia to Middle Egypt. The "typical" Pan-Grave assemblage is often described as a pan-shaped grave, sometimes surrounded by a loose ring of stones, containing a body buried in a flexed position with distinctive ceramics, jewelry, decorated bucrania, and leather goods (Bietak 1966; Cohen 1992; de Souza 2013; Liszka 2012). Due to their sudden appearance, especially in Upper Egypt in the late Middle Kingdom through the Second Intermediate Period, as well as the weaponry found in their burials, the Pan-Grave were identified as mercenaries serving in the Theban army (de Souza 2013, pp. 109–110; Ryholt 1997, pp. 178–179). They were also equated with the Medjay of contemporary Egyptian texts, but this link has been convincingly challenged (Liszka 2012, 2015).

Several recent studies into the Pan-Grave Culture have shown significant variation in the expression of this potential identity within the Egyptian Nile Valley. Generally, the southernmost cemeteries tend to align more with the "typical" assemblage, featuring round pit graves and contracted burials, while more northerly sites feature rectangular graves with supine inhumations. This shift to a more traditionally Egyptian form of burial, along with the inclusion of Egyptian funerary objects such as kohl pots, storage jars, and occasionally coffins, has been explained as the Egyptianization of these immigrants (de Souza 2013, p. 112). However, upon closer examination, the incorporation of these Egyptian elements did not come at the expense of the inclusion of standard Pan-Grave artifacts and ceramics within these "Egyptianized" graves. Though Cohen and de Souza disagree as to the chronological significance of this change in burial practice, they agree that the maintenance of some Pan-Grave customs in all the graves is crucial to demonstrate individual agency in selecting from amongst both traditions (Cohen 1992; de Souza 2013). As de Souza emphasizes, "If funeral rituals are interpreted as an effort to reaffirm the identity of the deceased, then the strong Nubian character of the assemblages is a clear indication that the Pan-Grave community retained a strong and distinct identity" (de Souza 2013, p. 118). Although it remains unclear why these burials ceased in the New Kingdom, it was seemingly not due to overwhelming Egyptianization.

Many further distinctions have also been recognized within Pan-Grave Culture. Bourriau classified a split in the Egyptian ceramics found at these sites; those at Deir el Rifeh follow the Lower Egyptian tradition, while those at contemporary Mostagedda, just a few miles south and across the river, follow the Upper Egyptian tradition. She proposed that this division could be explained by different political alliances with the Hyksos and Thebans, respectively (Bourriau 1990, pp. 44–46). Additionally, in an extensive examination of Pan-Grave ceramics, de Souza identifies at least five, if not more, regional variations on the manifestation of Pan-Grave Culture, suggesting that we instead consider the Pan-Grave as a cultural horizon. He rightly argues that given these were likely nomadic bands, each would have had their own identities and expressions thereof, and would have been exposed to different interaction and exchange influences (de Souza 2019, pp. 140–153). Consequently, what has previously been treated as a homogenous immigrant identity actually has a variety of divisions, demonstrating that borders and bordering processes can occur within the borderland as well.

5.3 The Oases

The Western Desert of Egypt was home to various nomadic groups, but permanent settlement was only supported in the largest oases, namely Siwa, Bahariya, Farafra, Dakhleh, and Kharga. Even the closest of these oases were a several-day journey from the Nile Valley, necessitating appropriate preparation and a stock of water and supplies (Giddy 1987). This broad region was always a borderland, a zone of intense interaction between "Egyptians" (or people from the valley) – who were the immigrants in this case – and local desert groups. Interestingly, throughout pharaonic history, terms for the oases were almost always determined by the $ḫ3st$ sign, and the inhabitants of the oases were called $wḥ3tyw$, "oasis dwellers," which also received the $ḫ3st$ and throw stick classifiers, as on the Middle Kingdom stela of Ikudidi (Gauthier 1925, pp. 202–229). In New Kingdom tomb scenes, these oasians are depicted with specific dress and hair, further distinguishing them from the other groups shown. Two Third Intermediate Period texts, the Maunier Stela and the Tale of Woe, portrayed the oases as decidedly unpleasant and places for criminal banishment. This consistency in representation demonstrates that the oases and their inhabitants were thought of as foreign (Hubschmann 2010b, pp. 52–58; Morris 2010a). This case study focuses on the oases because they retained a distinct borderland identity despite constant contact with and periodic occupation by the Egyptian state.

One of the key concerns of research in this area is the constantly changing level of pharaonic presence and (claimed?) control over the oases. Early Dynastic serekhs, inscribed at the mouths of wadis along the valley route and at Kharga, are the earliest evidence for Egyptian presence in the region, likely in the form of royal expeditions. Such marking implies that the Egyptians "saw themselves as not of this region" and sought to incorporate it ideologically into the new state (Hamilton 2019, pp. 161–164). Starting in this period, and increasing in the Third–Fourth Dynasties, sites like Mut al-Kharab in Dakhleh show a combination of Nile Valley ceramics and those of the local Sheikh Muftah Cultural Unit. This evidence has been interpreted as the start of Egyptian colonization of the oases, primarily for resource exploitation, in which immigrant Egyptians lived alongside indigenous groups (Hope & Kaper 2010, p. 220; Ricketts 2020, pp. 599–602). While the material culture of the oases during the later Old Kingdom shows all the hallmarks of material entanglement and hybridity, some sites show a maintained spatial separation between traditions while others do not, and both groups retain clear markers of distinction (Ricketts 2020), exemplifying a range of interactive strategies and outcomes.

By the late Sixth Dynasty, an Egyptian administration was set up at Ayn Asil/Balat in Dakhleh, which kept in contact with the central government at Memphis (Pantalacci 2013). According to the autobiography of Khentikaupepy, the officials in charge would have been raised at the court in Memphis and appointed personally by the king (Pantalacci 2013, p. 199). Many material elements emphasized their ties to the valley. They had large mastabas and material culture similar to the valley, as well as evidence for the royal cults of Pepi I and II (Hubschmann 2010b, pp. 60–63; Morris 2010a, p. 139; Pantalacci 2013, p. 201). Their "palace" contained an archive whose texts were written in Egyptian, but were inscribed on clay tablets rather than papyri, a unique occurrence (Pantalacci 2013, p. 197).

In fact, while these administrators worked for the Egyptian king and likely came from the Nile Valley, numerous elements from Balat indicate they held the power, royal favor, or simple distance from the king needed to do things differently, in a way endemic to this borderland. The official in charge was the *ḥḳꜣ wḥꜣt*, the "Ruler of the Oasis," rather than the more standard titles for district leaders within the Nile Valley (Valloggia 1985). The unique title *ḥḳ₃* was more commonly applied to the leaders of foreign lands, people with direct authority over their region (Pantalacci 2013, p. 199). These rulers were also granted *ka* chapels and cults by a decree of Pepi II, a prerogative normally reserved for the king himself (Moeller 2018, p. 182; Morris 2010a, p. 139; Pantalacci 2013, p. 201). Writing occurred on clay tablets, a fact that may have resulted from a lack of resources, but was still a practice specific to this borderland. Hardtke even argued that the occurrence of extended family members within the administration of the oases demonstrated a kinship-based structure distinct from the Nile Valley (Hardtke 2020, p. 243). Consequently, by the late Old Kingdom, the oases, especially Dakhleh, represented a liminal zone in which novel cultural production and new practices were formed.

The oases continued to be a unique "third space" throughout pharaonic history, even during periods when the Egyptian king supposedly held more direct control. In a royal inscription from Deir el-Ballas, Montuhotep II claims that he annexed both Wawat and the oases to Upper Egypt (Darnell 2008; Fischer 1957, p. 40). Darnell proposed that this was the first time the oases were officially incorporated into the Egyptian state (Darnell 2008, p. 100). Yet only a few reigns later, private stelae recorded trouble. The stelae of Kay and Dd-Iqw both reported being sent by Senwosret I to put down rebellions in the oases (Darnell 2008, p. 101; Fischer 1957, p. 41; Hope & Kaper 2010, p. 231). Even once this region was supposedly quelled, local leaders still took advantage of their borderland context to flaunt their unique authority. The stela of Sa-Igai, a governor of Dakhleh, has been dated to the reign of Montuhotep II. The inscription not only names him as Chief of the Priests, but also a *ḥḳ₃*, perhaps referencing the Old Kingdom borderland title. Further, it claims that Sa-Igai erected monuments for the borderland-specific cult of Igai, "Lord of the Oasis" (Hope & Kaper 2010, pp. 227–228; Kaper 2020, p. 370; Morris 2010a, p. 140), making it perhaps the earliest record of the public patronage of temples, an act that had previously been a solely royal honor (Hope & Kaper 2010). Later, potentially during the reign of Senwosret III, two governors of Dakhleh, Ameny and Mery, depicted themselves in rock art sporting hairstyles and belts decorated with uraei, another royal prerogative (Hardtke 2020, p. 243; Tallet 2020, p. 707).

Through the Third Intermediate and Late Periods, the oases continued to express a distinctive, borderland culture characterized by entanglement. A particularly interesting case comes from a small temple to Amun of Ighespep in Al Bahrein, an uninhabited oasis outside of Siwa, dating to the reign of Nectanebo I (Figure 18). The decorative program of this small monument is incredibly unusual; while polychrome offering scenes focus on

Figure 18 Wenamun offering to Amun of Ighespep, Al Bahrein – by author after Gallo 2006, figure 12.

specifically oasian deities, only the eastern half of the temple features Nectanebo. The Egyptian king is shown in standard pharaonic costume with the titles *s₃ rꜥ* and *nsw bity*. However, on the western walls of the temple, the offering is being performed by an individual named Wenamun, who wears a headband with a vertical feather, typically a marker of Western Desert identities. Paralleling Nectanebo, Wenamun receives royal titles and cartouches; he is called "King of Upper and Lower Egypt and of the feather" as well as "the powerful one of the two deserts of Chou" (Gallo 2006; Hardtke 2020, pp. 246–248). In this setting, Wenamun is shown as equal to Nectanebo, simply a contemporary ruler with equivalent titles specific to this borderland. This example demonstrates the fluidity and flexibility of borderland identities, as Wenamun selects from among the repertoires both of Egypt and the oases to communicate his local role and authority. The reference to the two deserts of Chou also echoes the term "the two lands of the Oases," which indicated the unity of the Northern (Baharia and Farafra) and Southern Oases (Kharga and Dakhleh) (Gauthier 1925, pp. 27–28). The unification of duality in these terms reflects the same concept seen in Egyptian geographic labels and titles, like the two lands, Upper and Lower Egypt, and the two banks (Kuhlmann 2013). Therefore, Wenamun's employment of both of these titles in particular shows his borderland adaptation of Egyptian traditions.

5.4 The Eastern Delta

The final case study, the region of the Eastern Delta, shares numerous aspects with the other borderlands discussed. First, interaction between locals and Southwest Asians, as well as continuous mobility, was a constant characteristic of this zone. Trade and resource expeditions were launched from the region by both land and sea, ensuring the focus of this borderland was oriented to the Mediterranean and West Asia. Multidirectional immigration between the Eastern Delta and West Asia is attested as early as the Predynastic Period (Van den Brink & Levy 2002), causing the area to retain a unique borderland identity distinct in many ways from the Nile Valley. Second, the politico-ideological border shifted frequently throughout pharaonic history; sources like P. Anastasi IV refer to Piramesse as the site of the border between the Egypt and West Asia, while multiple texts indicate that Avaris may not have been considered a part of Egypt during certain eras (see Section 2.4; Candelora 2019a).

It is becoming increasingly clear that bordering processes occurred within this borderland as well; in the Second Intermediate Period, distinct expressions of hybridity and identity can be found not only in different places within the Eastern Delta, such as the sites in Wadi Tumilat (Mourad 2021, pp. 76–83), but even in different excavation areas within the regional capital at Tell el Dab'a. For example, the settlement in Area F/I displayed a blend of material culture that drew from both Egyptian and West Asian traditions. Houses, which were of typical Egyptian layout, had attached, aboveground burial chambers identified as totenhauser with remains of family burials and cultic activity apparently centered on an adult male. While both cultures practiced ancestor veneration, Müller argued that these installations and their location within the settlement more closely align with West Asian burial customs, but the fact that these vaults were accessible only from outside, rather than from within the house, indicated the incorporation of Egyptian notions of separation between the living and dead. This particular admixture resulted in a new tradition specific not just to the Eastern Delta borderland, but to this area of the city in particular. Additionally, the visibility of these vaults, as well as a potential communal chapel surrounded by further inhumations, were outward expressions of group solidarity – a bordering process – that served to created a unique identity (Müller 2015).

Roughly 500 meters to the southeast, Area A/II exhibits different burial traditions. Burial styles and the nature of this area changed over time, displaying hyperlocal adjustments to altered circumstances. In the late Middle Kingdom strata G/1–3, only eight subterranean tombs were excavated featuring generally "Egyptian"-style architecture, but some melding of other aspects, such as body position, ceramics, and burial goods, with Southwest Asian types (Bader 2021, pp. 53–54). In stratum F, the area was converted from a settlement to a sacred complex with a massive temple (Temple III) and cemetery, in which all the tombs were aligned to the temple. In the following phases, the settlement expanded back across the area, preserving the temple, and the material culture apparently underwent a noticeable shift to a hybrid "Delta type" inspired by both Egyptian and Southwest Asian cultures. In the latest Hyksos phase, new tomb types were introduced featuring shafts attached to houses, leading to subterranean family tombs (Forstner-Müller 2010, p. 129). Overall, the burials in Area A/II reflect the constantly shifting significance of the area, adapting to the conditions and/or demographics of each new phase. Distinctly unlike the visible funerary structures of area F/I however, the tombs in Area A/II from all strata lack superstructures (Forstner-Müller 2010, p. 130), indicating different burial practices and meanings in this nearby area demarcating a potential border within the larger city.

Bietak has suggested that the westernmost Complex 1 in Area R/III was a settlement of purely Egyptians, whereas Complexes 2 and 3 across the street were occupied by Southwest Asians, according to the presence versus absence of toggle pins and intramural burials (Bietak 2016, pp. 269–272). However, it is more likely that Complex 1 served as an administrative district, as first proposed by the excavators, and it is crucial to consider that in a borderland context such as this, toggle pins may not represent such firm "ethnic markers," but instead reflect material and relational entanglements linked to fluid identities (Bader 2021, p. 92).

Even the immigrant-descended rulers of the Fifteenth Dynasty recognized and accommodated the variability of the borderland community over which they ruled. They strategically maintained aspects of their Southwest Asian origins while incorporating and adapting elements from Egyptian traditions, in many cases creating a third, Delta-specific mode of doing. They commissioned monumental inscriptions in hieroglyphs, including standard Egyptian royal titulary and throne names. However, they preserved their personal, Semitic names in a cartouche, an archetypal symbol of Egyptian kingship, and selected an Egyptian title, *ḥḳꜣ ḫꜣswt*, to emphasize their foreign backgrounds. In terms of their governing structure, the Hyksos seem to have retained their kinship-based power networks, but overlaid Egyptian titles and tools, such as scarab seals and the language itself, to produce an administration specific to the borderland. They continued to participate in Southwest Asian networks of trade and diplomacy via gift-giving and correspondence, granting them access to both political allies and a rich supply of desirable imports. Additionally, the Hyksos adopted aspects of Egyptian religion, claiming to be sons and embodiments of Re, instructed by Thoth, and beloved of Sobek. Yet they also chose a syncretized borderland deity – Seth of Avaris, a union of Seth and a Southwest Asian storm god – as their patron, and established a temple and cult to him that would continue in this liminal region for more than 400 years. The persistence of this distinct borderland identity was made apparent when the Ramesside kings, themselves members of this borderland community, adopted the same god as their own royal patron, and further established the cults of other Southwest Asian deities at Piramesse (Candelora 2017, 2019a).

6 Conclusions: Immigrant Impacts

It is crucial to consider the term "border" as both a noun and a verb – a thing and a process (Diener & Hagen 2012, p. 59). The paradox of studying borders in this way is that they both create divisions and invite interaction across them (Baud & Van Schendel 1997, p. 216). In the case of ancient Egypt, approaching the borderlands as the core space rather than the periphery helps mute the overbearing foreigner topos of state rhetoric and the anachronistic imposition of a national, Egyptian identity. Instead, it allows for the examination and nuancing of the lived reality of both immigrants and locals in these interaction zones. Further, borderlands encourage us to embrace ambiguity as the state of the question, rather than approaching these topics through false objectivity. In these regions where there was never a "precontact" or "culturally pure" phase, identity and immigration remained flexible, multidirectional concepts. Material culture and practices blended, reflecting a hybridized form of production, and cultures were consciously juxtaposed as a form of bordering between groups. It is also becoming apparent with new research that bordering processes defined distinct, locally focused identities within the borderland as well, regardless of whether that liminal zone was located at the assumed edges of Egypt or in the heart of the Nile Valley.

Ancient Egypt was characterized by the vagueness and permeability of its borders and by a lack of isolation. Interaction and immigration were constants throughout pharaonic history, only increasing in intensity as time went on. This is not meant to imply that the numbers of immigrants were necessarily large, but that their infusion into and inclusion in Egyptian society was common, and that even small-scale interactions could have far-reaching effects. Critically, acculturation is not a process only the immigrants undergo in such contact scenarios. Members of the host society can and do acculturate aspects of immigrant culture, usually due to a desire to be slightly unique for status and upward social mobility (Rudmin *et al.* 2007, p. 50). This also raises the question of when foreigners and foreign cultural elements cease to be alien (Panagiotopoulos 2012), as well as what aspects of archetypal Egyptian culture are in fact the negotiated cultural production of a borderland.

Many different aspects of Egyptian culture were impacted by cross-border interaction or the integration of immigrants into society. Much of the innovations that characterized the New Kingdom, for example, were driven by accommodations and transformations of material and nonmaterial aspects of culture in borderland contexts, both within and beyond Egypt. The incorporation and adaptation of these cultural elements were not simple, one-to-one correspondences or unidirectional inheritances, but the result of complex negotiation and bordering processes that altered Egyptian society from the religious and political to the militaristic and mundane. Foreign deities were not just added into the Egyptian pantheon, but were entangled in Egyptian mythological traditions, and in the case of Qedeshet, for instance, deities were invented anew from a blend of religious influences to suit the circumstances and communities of their time (Cornelius 2004; Mourad 2021; Schneider 2011; Zivie-Coche 2018). Cuisine was transformed by the importation of foreign foods and domesticated crops, as well as the associated knowledge of production – an excellent example being that of wine and viticulture. Yet the impact of these foods (or drinks) was not restricted solely to the realm of diet and farming, but reverberated also into religious ritual and burial practice. Wine in particular remained a borderland product in several ways; its cultivation was better suited to the Delta and oases, and immigrant vintners were brought into Egypt throughout at least the New Kingdom (Lesko 1996; Murray 2000). A vast array of technologies were adapted for Egyptian use from such borderland encounters, from the most basic system of weights and measures to the complex military package featuring the chariot, horse, composite bow, and scale armor. These technologies touched most facets of Egyptian life, including simple commodity exchange, household weaving, transport, laboring with tools, music, and much more (Mourad 2021, pp. 219–348; Shaw 2012). The military was the social arena that was perhaps most transformed; not just the material elements of new weapons, armor, and machines, but also tactics, jargon, and even military reward systems were adapted to local needs through the continual integration of immigrant soldiers and craftsmen within the Egyptian military. Additional nonmaterial transformations occurred in the language, diplomatic practice, and even cultural values (Candelora 2019a; Moreno García 2024, p. 17).

Therefore, envisioning ancient Egyptian borderlands as particularly dynamic social spheres "in which interaction and change can occur more readily than elsewhere" (Feuer 2016, p. 21) allows us to separate the study of borders from geopolitics. Rather than exploring borders as restrictive, linear structures, approaching them as contact zones emphasizes the transboundary mobility, exchange, and mutual production that occurs within these spaces. These borderlands are no longer delegated to the fringes of the map or of society, but instead center the flexibility and accommodation of these liminal spaces in the construction of identity and innovation.

Works Cited

Abbas, M. R. (2017). A Survey of the Military Role of the Sherden Warriors in the Egyptian Army during the Ramesside Period. *Égypte Nilotique et Méditerranéenne*, **10**, 7–23.

Adams, W. Y. (1984). *Nubia: Corridor to Africa*, Princeton, NJ: Princeton University Press.

Adelman, J., & Aron, S. (1999). From Borderlands to Borders: Empires, Nation-States, and the Peoples in between in North American History. *American Historical Review*, **104**(3), 814–841.

Agnew, J. (1994). The Territorial Trap: The Geographical Assumptions of International Relations Theory. *Review of International Political Economy*, **1**(1), 53–80.

Alba, R., & Nee, V. (1997). Rethinking Assimilation Theory for a New Era of Immigration. *International Migration Review*, **31**(4), 826–874.

Alba, R., & Nee, V. (2003). *Remaking the American Mainstream: Assimilation and Contemporary Immigration*, Cambridge, MA: Harvard University Press.

Allen, J. P. (2010). *Middle Egyptian: An Introduction to the Language and Culture of Hieroglyphs*, 2nd edition, Cambridge: Cambridge University Press.

Allen, J. P. (2014). *Middle Egyptian Literature: Eight Literary Works of the Middle Kingdom*, Cambridge: Cambridge University Press.

Amilhat Szary, A.-L. (2015). Borders and Boundaries. In J. Agnew, A. Secor, J. Sharpe, & V. Mamadouh, eds., *Handbook of Political Geography*, London: Wiley-Blackwell, pp. 13–25.

Anderson, B. (2006). *Imagined Communities: Reflections on the Origin and Spread of Nationalism*, London: Verso.

Anzaldúa, G. (1987). *Borderlands/La Frontera: The New Mestiza*, San Francisco, CA: Aunt Lute Books.

Assmann, J. (1990). *Ma'at: Gerechtigkeit und Unsterblichkeit im alten Ägypten*, Munich: Beck.

Assmann, J. (1996). Zum Konzept der Fremdheit im alten Ägypten. In M. Schuster, ed., *Die Begegnung mit dem Fremden: Wertungen und Wirkungen in Hochkulturen vom Altertum bis zur Gegenwart*, Stuttgart: Teubner, pp. 77–99.

Assmann, J. (2003). *The Mind of Egypt: History and Meaning in the Time of the Pharaohs* (A. Jenkins, trans.), Cambridge, MA: Harvard University Press.

Bader, B. (2011). Traces of Foreign Settlers in the Archaeological Record of Tell el-Dab'a/Egypt. In K. Duistermaat & I. Regulski, eds., *Intercultural Contacts in the Ancient Mediterranean*, Leuven: Peeters, pp. 127–148.

Bader, B. (2012). Migration in Archaeology: An Overview with a Focus on Ancient Egypt. In M. Messer, R. Schroder, & R. Wodak, eds., *Migrations: Interdisciplinary Perspectives*, Vienna: Springer, pp. 213–226.

Bader, B. (2021). *Material Culture and Identities in Egyptology: Towards a Better Understanding of Cultural Encounters and Their Influence on Material Culture*, Vienna: Austrian Academy of Sciences Press.

Barnard, H. (2008). Maps and mapmaking in Ancient Egypt. In H. Selin, ed., *Encyclopaedia of the History of Science, Technology, and Medicine in Non-Western Cultures*, Vol. II, Dordrecht: Springer, pp. 1273–1276.

Barnard, H. (2013). The Desert Hinterland of Qasr Ibrim. In J. van der Vliet & J. L. Hagen, eds., *Qasr Ibrim, Between Egypt and Africa*, Leiden: Nederlands Instituut voor het Nabije Oosten. pp. 83–103.

Barnard, H., & Duistermaat, K. (eds.). (2012). *The History of the Peoples of the Eastern Desert*, Los Angeles, CA: Cotsen Institute of Archaeology Press.

Barnard, H., & Wendrich, W. (eds.). (2008). *The Archaeology of Mobility: Old World and New World Nomadism*, Los Angeles, CA: Cotsen Institute of Archaeology Press.

Barth, F. (1969). *Ethnic Groups and Boundaries: The Social Organization of Culture Difference*, 1998 Edition. Long Grove, IL: Waveland Press.

Baud, M., & Van Schendel, W. (1997). Toward a Comparative History of Borderlands. *Journal of World History*, **8**(2), 211–242.

Becking, B. (2022). The Identity of the People at Elephantine. In M. Folmer, ed., *Elephantine Revisited: New Insights into the Judean Community and Its Neighbors*, University Park: Pennsylvania State University Press, pp. 106–123.

Bentley, G. C. (1987). Ethnicity and Practice. *Comparative Studies in Society and History*, **29**(1), 24–55.

Berry, J. W. (1997). Immigration, Acculturation, and Adaptation. *Applied Psychology: An International Review*, **46**(1), 5–34.

Bhabha, H. K. (1994). *The Location of Culture*, London: Routledge.

Biersteker, T. J., & Weber, C. (eds.). (1996). *State Sovereignty as Social Construct*, Cambridge: Cambridge University Press.

Bietak, M. (1966). *Ausgrabungen in Sayala-Nubien 1961–1965: Denkmäler der C-Gruppe und der Pan-Gräber-Kultur*, Vienna: Austrian Academy of Sciences.

Bietak, M. (2010). From Where Came the Hyksos and Where Did They Go? In M. Marée, ed., *The Second Intermediate Period (Thirteenth–Seventeenth*

Dynasties): Current Research, Future Prospects, Leuven: Peeters, pp. 139–181.

Bietak, M. (2016). The Egyptian Community in Avaris during the Hyksos Period. *Ägypten und Levante*, **26**, 263–274.

Bissonnette, A., & Vallet, E. (eds.). (2022). *Borders and Border Walls: Insecurity, Symbolism, Vulnerabilities*, London: Routledge.

Bleiberg, E. (1984). Aspects of Political, Religious and Economic Basis of Ancient Egyptian Imperialism during the New Kingdom (PhD Thesis), University of Toronto.

Bonnett, A. (2014). *Unruly Places: Lost Spaces, Secret Cities, and Other Inscrutable Geographies*, Boston, MA: Houghton Mifflin Harcourt.

Bourdieu, P. (1977). *Outline of a Theory of Practice*, Cambridge: Cambridge University Press.

Bourriau, J. (1990). Some Archaeological Notes on the Kamose Texts. In A. Leahy & J. Tait, eds., *Studies on Ancient Egypt in Honour of H. S. Smith*, London: Egypt Exploration Society, pp. 44–46.

Broekman, G. P. F. (2009). Falcon-Headed Coffins and Cartonnages. *Journal of Egyptian Archaeology*, **95**(1), 67–81.

Broekman, G. P. F. (2010). Libyan Rule over Egypt: The Influence of the Tribal Background of the Ruling Class on Political Structures and Developments during the Libyan Period in Egypt. *Studien zur altägyptischen Kultur*, **39**, 85–99.

Broekman, G. P. F., Demarée, R. J., & Kaper, O. E. (eds.). (2009). *The Libyan Period in Egypt: Historical and Cultural Studies into the 21st–24th Dynasties: Proceedings of a Conference at Leiden University, 25–27 October 2007*, Leiden: Peeters.

Buzon, M. R., & Bowen, G. J. (2010). Oxygen and Carbon Isotope Analysis of Human Tooth Enamel from the New Kingdom Site of Tombos in Nubia. *Archaeometry*, **52**(5), 855–868.

Buzon, M. R., & Simonetti, A. (2013). Strontium Isotope ($87Sr/86Sr$) Variability in the Nile Valley: Identifying Residential Mobility during Ancient Egyptian and Nubian Sociopolitical Changes in the New Kingdom and Napatan Periods. *American Journal of Physical Anthropology*, **151**(1), 1–9.

Buzon, M. R., Simonetti, A., & Creaser, R. A. (2007). Migration in the Nile Valley during the New Kingdom Period: A Preliminary Strontium Isotope Study. *Journal of Archaeological Science*, **34**(9), 1391–1401.

Candelora, D. (2017). Defining the Hyksos: A Reevaluation of the Title HqA xAswt and Its Implications for Hyksos Identity. *Journal of the American Research Center in Egypt*, **53**, 203–221.

Candelora, D. (2019a). The Eastern Delta as a Middle Ground for Hyksos Identity Negotiation. *Mitteilungen des Deutschen Archäologischen Instituts, Abteilung Kairo*, **75**, 77–94.

Candelora, D. (2019b). Hybrid Military Communities of Practice: The Integration of Immigrants as the Catalyst for Egyptian Social Transformation in the 2nd Millennium. In J. Mynářová, S. Alivernini, D. Bělohoubková, & M. Kilani, eds., *A Stranger in the House: The Crossroads III. Proceedings of an International Conference on Foreigners in Ancient Egyptian and Near Eastern Societies of the Bronze Age held in Prague, September 10–13, 2018*, Prague: Czech Institute of Egyptology, pp. 25–48.

Candelora, D. (2020). Redefining the Hyksos: Immigration and Identity Negotiation in the Second Intermediate Period (PhD Dissertation), University of California, Los Angeles.

Candelora, D. (2022a). The Egyptianization of Egypt and Egyptology: Exploring Identity in Ancient Egypt. In D. Candelora, N. Ben-Marzouk, & K. M. Cooney, eds., *Ancient Egyptian Society: Challenging Assumptions, Exploring Approaches*, London: Routledge, pp. 103–110.

Candelora, D. (2022b). Shifting Boundaries, Conflicting Perspectives: (Re)establishing the Borders of Kemet through Variable Social Identities. In D. Candelora, N. Ben-Marzouk, & K. M. Cooney, eds., *Ancient Egyptian Society: Challenging Assumptions, Exploring Approaches*, London: Routledge, pp. 235–247.

Candelora, D. (2023). Religion Materialized: Identity and Built Religious Space at Tell el Dab'a. In S. R. Steadman & N. Laneri, eds., *Material Religion in the Ancient Near East and Egypt*, London: Bloomsbury, pp. 119–128.

Castronovo, R. (1997). Compromised Narratives along the Border: The Mason–Dixon Line, Resistance, and Hegemony. In S. Michaelsen & D. E. Johnson, eds., *Border Theory: The Limits of Cultural Politics*, Minneapolis: University of Minnesota Press, pp. 195–220.

Černý, J. (1939). *Late Ramesside Letters*, Brussels: Fondation Égyptologique Reine Élisabeth.

Chantrain, G. (2019). About "Egyptianity" and "Foreignness" in Egyptian Texts: A Context-Sensitive Lexical Study. In J. Mynářová, S. Alivernini, D. Bělohoubková, & M. Kilani, eds., *The Crossroads III – A Stranger in the House: Foreigners and Ancient Egyptian and Near Eastern Societies of the Bronze Age*, Prague: Czech Institute of Egyptology, pp. 49–72.

Cohen, E. S. (1992). Egyptianization and the Acculturation Hypothesis: An Investigation of the Pan-Grave, Kerman and C-Group Material Cultures in Egypt and the Sudan during the Second Intermediate Period and Eighteenth Dynasty (PhD Dissertation), Yale University.

Colburn, H. P. (2020). Udjahorresnet the Persian: Being an Essay on the Archaeology of Identity. *Journal of Ancient Egyptian Interconnections*, **26**, 59–74.

Cole, E. M. (2015). Foreign Influence in the Late New Kingdom and Third Intermediate Period. In M. Pinarello, J. Yoo, J. Lundock, & C. Walsh, eds., *Current Research in Egyptology 2014: Proceedings of the Fifteenth Annual Symposium*, Oxford: Oxbow Books, pp. 113–123.

Cooney, J. D. (1954). The Portrait of an Egyptian Collaborator. *Brooklyn Museum Bulletin*, **15**(2), 1–16.

Cooney, W. (2011). Egypt's Encounter with the West: Race, Culture and Identity (PhD Dissertation), Durham University.

Cooper, J. (2015). Toponymy on the Periphery: Placenames of the Eastern Desert, Red Sea, and South Sinai in Egyptian Documents from the Early Dynastic until the End of the New Kingdom (PhD Dissertation), Macquarie University.

Cornelius, I. (1994). *The Iconography of the Canaanite Gods Reshef and Ba'al: Late Bronze and Iron Age I periods (C 1500–1000 BCE)*, Fribourg: Vandenhoeck & Ruprecht.

Cornelius, I. (2004). *The Many Faces of the Goddess: The Iconography of the Syro-Palestinian Goddesses Anat, Astarte, Qedeshet, and Asherah c. 1500–1000 BCE*, Fribourg: Vandenhoeck & Ruprecht.

Darnell, J. C. (2007). The Deserts. In T. A. H. Wilkinson, ed., *The Egyptian World*, Abingdon: Routledge, pp. 29–48.

Darnell, J. C. (2008). The Eleventh Dynasty Royal Inscription from Deir el-Ballas [Planches VIII–IX]. *Revue d'Égyptologie*, **59**, 81–110.

Darnell, J. C. (2021). *Egypt and the Desert*, Cambridge: Cambridge University Press.

Davies, W. V. (2017). Nubia in the New Kingdom: The Egyptians at Kurgus. In N. Spencer, A. Stevens, & M. Binder, eds., *Nubia in the New Kingdom: Lived Experience, Pharaonic Control and Indigenous Traditions*, Leuven: Peeters, pp. 65–105.

de Leon, J. (2015). *The Land of Open Graves: Living and Dying on the Migrant Trail*, Oakland: University of California Press.

de Souza, A. (2013). The Egyptianisation of the Pan-Grave Culture: A New Look at an Old Idea. *Bulletin of the Australian Centre for Egyptology*, **24**, 109–126.

de Souza, A. (2019). *New Horizons: The Pan-Grave Ceramic Tradition in Context*, London: Golden House.

de Souza, A. (2020). Melting Pots: Entanglement, Appropriation, Hybridity, and Assertive Objects between the Pan-Grave and Egyptian Ceramic Traditions. *Journal of Ancient Egyptian Interconnections*, **27**, 1–23.

di Biase-Dyson, C. (2013). *Foreigners and Egyptians in the Late Egyptian Stories: Linguistic, Literary and Historical Perspectives*, Leiden: Brill.

Diener, A. C., & Hagen, J. (2012). *Borders: A Very Short Introduction*, Oxford: Oxford University Press.

Dietler, M. (1998). Consumption, Agency, and Cultural Entanglement: Theoretical Implications of a Mediterranean Colonial Encounter. In J. G. Cusick, ed., *Studies in Culture Contact: Interaction, Culture Change, and Archaeology*, Carbondale: Southern Illinois University Press, pp. 288–315.

Dietler, M. (2010). *Archaeologies of Colonialism*, Oakland: University of California Press.

Doty, R. L. (1996). Sovereignty and the Nation: Constructing the Boundaries of National Identity. In T. J. Biersteker & C. Weber, eds., *State Sovereignty as Social Construct*, Cambridge: Cambridge University Press, pp. 121–147.

Dunand, F., & Zivie-Coche, C. (2005). *Gods and Men in Egypt: 3000 BCE to 395 CE* (D. Lorton, Trans.), Ithaca, NY: Cornell University Press.

Dunham, D., & Janssen, J. (1960). *Second Cataract Forts Volume 1: Semna Kumma*, Boston, MA: Museum of Fine Arts.

El-Enany, N. (2020). *Bordering Britain: Law, Race and Empire*, Manchester: Manchester University Press.

Emanuel, J. (2013). "Šrdn from the Sea": The Arrival, Integration, and Acculturation of a "Sea People." *Journal of Ancient Egyptian Interconnections*, **5**(1), 14–27.

Emberling, G. (1997). Ethnicity in Complex Societies: Archaeological Perspectives. *Journal of Archaeological Research*, **5**(4), 295–344.

Eyre, C. J. (1990). The Semna Stelae: Quotation, Genre, and Functions of Literature. In S. Israelit-Groll, ed., *Studies in Egyptology Presented to Miriam Lichtheim*, Vol. 1, Jerusalem: The Magnes Press, The Hebrew University, pp. 134–165.

Feuer, B. (2016). *Boundaries, Borders and Frontiers in Archaeology: A Study of Spatial Relationships*, Jefferson, NC: McFarland.

Fischer, H. G. (1957). A God and a General of the Oasis on a Stela of the Late Middle Kingdom. *Journal of Near Eastern Studies*, **16**(4), 223–235.

Förster, F., & Riemer, H. (2013). *Desert Road Archaeology in Ancient Egypt and Beyond*, Cologne: Heinrich-Barth-Institut.

Forstner-Müller, I. (2008). *Tell el-Dabʿa XVI: Die Gräber des Areals A/II von Tell el-Dabʿa*, Vienna: Österreichische Akademie der Wissenschaften.

Forstner-Müller, I. (2010). Tombs and Burial Customs at Tell el-Dab'a during the Late Middle Kingdom and the Second Intermediate Period. In M. Marée, ed., *The Second Intermediate Period (Thirteenth–Seventeenth Dynasties): Current Research, Future Prospects*, Leuven: Peeters, pp. 127–138.

Frankfort, H. (1948). *Ancient Egyptian Religion: An Interpretation*, New York: Columbia University Press.

Gabaccia, D. R. (1999). Is Everywhere Nowhere? Nomads, Nations, and the Immigrant Paradigm of United States History. *Journal of American History*, **86**(3), 1115–1134.

Galán, J. M. (1995). *Victory and Border: Terminology Related to Egyptian Imperialism in the XVIIIth Dynasty*, Hildesheim: Gerstenberg.

Galán, J. M. (1999). The Egyptian Concept of Frontier. In L. Milano, S. de Martino, F. M. Fales, & G. B. Lanfranchi, eds., *Landscapes: Territories, Frontiers and Horizons in the Ancient Near East. Papers Presented to the XLIV Recontre Assyriologique Internationale, Venezia, 7–11 July 1997*, Padua: Sargon SRL.

Galczynski, J. (2024). The Egyptian Textile Industry: A Socio-historical Study of the Value of Textiles at the Intersection of Power and Identity during the New Kingdom (c. 1550–1070 BCE) (PhD Dissertation), University of California, Los Angeles.

Gallo, P. (2006). Ounamon, roi de l'oasis libyenne d'El-Bahreïn sous la XXXème dynastie. *Bulletin de la Société française d'égyptologie*, **166**, 11–30.

Gauthier, H. (1925). *Dictionnaire des Noms Géographiques Contenus dans les Textes Hiéroglyphiques*, Vol. I, Cairo: L'Institut Français d'Archéologie Orientale.

Giddy, L. L. (1987). *Egyptian Oases: Baḥariya, Dakhla, Farafra, and Kharga during Pharaonic Times*, Warminster: Aris & Phillips.

Gilroy, P. (1997). Diaspora and the Detours of Identity. In K. Woodward, ed., *Identity and Difference*, Vol. 3, London: Sage, pp. 301–344.

Gnirs, A. M. (1996). *Militär und Gesellschaft ein Beitrag zur Sozialgeschichte des Neuen Reiches*, Heidelberg: Heidelberger Orientverlag.

Goelet, O. (1999). Kemet and Other Egyptian Terms for Their Land. In R. Chazan, W. W. Hallo, & L. H. Schiffman, eds., *Ki Baruch Hu: Ancient Near Eastern, Biblical, and Judaic Studies in Honor of Baruch A. Levine*, University Park: Pennsylvania State University Press, pp. 23–42.

Goldberg-Ambrose, C. (1994). Of Native Americans and Tribal Members: The Impact of Law on Indian Group Life. *Law & Society Review*, **28**(5), 1123–1148.

Graeff, J. P. (2008). Kemet, Kemet über alles! Zu Patriotismus, Nationalismus und Rassismus im Alten Ägypten. In W. Waitkus, ed., *Diener des Horus. Festschrift für Dieter Kurth zum 65. Geburtstag*, Hamburg: PeWe, pp. 123–133.

Green, U. M., & Costion, K. E. (2017). Using a Graphic Model to Explore the Range of Cross-Cultural Interaction in Ancient Borderlands. In C. Beaule, ed., *Frontiers of Colonialism*, Gainesville: University Press of Florida, pp. 480–539.

Hafsaas-Tsakos, H. (2010). Between Kush and Egypt: The C-Group people of Lower Nubia during the Middle Kingdom and Second Intermediate Period. In W. Godlewski & A. Łajtar, eds., *Between the Cataracts: Proceedings of the 11th Conference of Nubian Studies Warsaw University, 27 August– 2 September 2006*, Vol. 2, Warsaw: Polish Center of Mediterranean Archaeology, pp. 389–396.

Hagen, F. (2007). Local Identities. In T. A. H. Wilkinson, ed., *The Egyptian World*, Abingdon: Routledge, pp. 242–251.

Hall, S. (1994). Cultural Identity and Diaspora. In P. Williams & L. Chrisman, eds., *Colonial Discourse and Post-colonial Theory*, Abingdon: Routledge.

Hämäläinen, P., & Truett, S. (2011). On Borderlands. *Journal of American History*, **98**(2), 338–361.

Hamilton, C. R. (2019). Egyptians as Foreigners in the Western Desert during the Early Dynastic Period. In J. Mynářová, M. Kilani, & S. Alivernini, eds., *A Stranger in the House – the Crossroads III: Proceedings of an International Conference on Foreigners in Ancient Egyptian and Near Eastern Societies of the Bronze Age Held in Prague, September 10–13, 2018*, Prague: Czech Institute of Egyptology, pp. 159–177.

Hardtke, F. E. (2020). The Long Reach of the Nile Valley: The Egyptianisation of Siwa and the Western Outer Oases. In A. R. Warfe, J. C. R. Gill, C. R. Hamilton, A. J. Pettman, & D. A. Stewart, eds., *Dust, Demons and Pots: Studies in Honour of Colin A. Hope*, Leuven: Peeters, pp. 241–256.

Haring, B. (2005). Occupation: Foreigner. Ethnic Difference and Integration in Pharaonic Egypt. In W. H. van Soldt, ed., *Ethnicity in Ancient Mesopotamia: Papers Read at the 48th Recontre Assyriologique Internationale Leiden, 1–4 July 2002*, Leiden: Nederlands Instituut voor het Nabije Oosten, pp. 162–172.

Hasdemir Bozkuş, G. (2023). City, Identity, Trade: An Observation on the Rise of Naukratis in the Archaic Period. *Phaselis*, **IX**, 65–85.

Hoch, J. E. (1994). *Semitic Words in Egyptian Texts of the New Kingdom and Third Intermediate Period*, Princeton, NJ: Princeton University Press.

Hodder, I. (2012). *Entangled: An Archaeology of the Relationships between Humans and Things*, Malden, MA: Wiley-Blackwell.

Hodgson, N. (2017). *Hadrian's Wall: Archaeology and History at the Limit of Rome's Empire*, Marlborough: Crowood Press.

Hope, C. A., & Kaper, O. E. (2010). A Governor of Dakhleh Oasis in the Early Middle Kingdom. In A. Woods, A. McFarlane, & S. Binder, eds., *Egyptian Culture and Society: Studies in Honour of Naguib Kanawati*, Cairo: Conseil Suprême des Antiquitiés, pp. 219–245.

Hornung, E. (1992). *Idea into Image: Essays on Ancient Egyptian Thought* (E. Bredeck, Trans.), New York: Timken.

Hubschmann, C. (2010a). Searching for the "Archaeologically Invisible": Libyans in Dakhleh Oasis in the Third Intermediate Period. *Journal of the American Research Center in Egypt*, **46**, 173–187.

Hubschmann, C. (2010b). Who Inhabited Dakhleh Oasis? Searching for an Oasis Identity in Pharaonic Egypt. *Papers from the Institute of Archaeology*, **20**, 51–66.

Irish, J. D., & Friedman, R. (2010). Dental Affinities of the C-Group Inhabitants of Hierakonpolis, Egypt: Nubian, Egyptian, or Both? *HOMO: Journal of Comparative Human Biology*, **61**(2), 81–101.

Jansen-Winkeln, K. (1999). Gab es in der alt ägyptischen Geschichte eine feudalistische Epoche? *Welt Des Orients*, **30**(7), 7–20.

Jansen-Winkeln, K. (2000). Die Fremdherrschaften in Ägypten im 1 Jahrtausend v. Chr. *Orientalia*, **69**, 1–20.

Johnson, J. H. (1999). Ethnic Considerations in Persian Period Egypt. In E. Teeter & J. A. Larson, eds., *Gold of Praise: Studies on Ancient Egypt in Honor of Edward F. Wente*, Chicago, IL: University of Chicago Press, pp. 211–222.

Jones, S. (1997). *The Archaeology of Ethnicity: Constructing Identities in the Past and Present*, London: Routledge.

Kaper, O. E. (2020). The God Seth in Dakhleh Oasis before the New Kingdom. In A. R. Warfe, J. C. R. Gill, C. R. Hamilton, A. J. Pettman, & D. A. Stewart, eds., *Dust, Demons and Pots: Studies in Honour of Colin A. Hope*, Leuven: Peeters, pp. 369–384.

Kees, H. (1934). Zu einigen Fachausdrücken der altägyptischen Provinzialverwaltung. *Zeitschrift für Ägyptische Sprache und Altertumskunde*, **70**(1), 83–91.

Kemp, B. J. (2006). *Ancient Egypt: Anatomy of a Civilization*, 2nd edition, London: Routledge.

Kemp, B. J. (2018). *Ancient Egypt: Anatomy of a Civilization*, 3rd edition, Abingdon: Routledge.

Kilani, M. (2015). Between Geographical Imaginary and Geographical Reality: Byblos and the Limits of the World in the 18th Dynasty. In M. Kilani, A. Belekdanian, C. Alvarez, S. Klein, & A. K. Gill, eds., *Current Research in Egyptology 2015: Proceedings of the Sixteenth Annual Symposium. University of Oxford 2015*, Oxford: Oxbow Books, pp. 74–87.

Kim, J. (2019). Ethnic Capital, Migration, and Citizenship: A Bourdieusian Perspective. *Ethnic and Racial Studies*, **42**(3), 357–385.

Kitchen, K. A. (1970). *Ramesside Inscriptions, Historical and Biographical*, Vol. II, Oxford: Blackwell.

Kitchen, K. A. (1990). The Arrival of the Libyans in Late New Kingdom Egypt. In A. Leahy, ed., *Libya and Egypt: c.1300–750 BC*, London: SOAS Centre of Near and Middle Eastern Studies and the Society for Libyan Studies, pp. 15–28.

Knapp, A. B. (2008). *Prehistoric and Protohistoric Cyprus: Identity, Insularity, and Connectivity*, Oxford: Oxford University Press.

Knapp, A. B. (2021). *Migration Myths and the End of the Bronze Age in the Eastern Mediterranean*, Cambridge: Cambridge University Press.

Knoblauch, C. (2019). Middle Kingdom Fortresses. In D. Raue, ed., *Handbook of Ancient Nubia*, Berlin: De Gruyter, pp. 367–392.

Kootz, A. (2013). State-Territory and Borders versus Hegemony and Its Installations: Imaginations Expressed by the Ancient Egyptians during the Classical Periods. In F. Jesse & C. Vogel, eds., *The Power of Walls: Fortifications in Ancient Northeastern Africa: Proceedings of the International Workshop held at the University of Cologne 4th–7th August 2011*, Cologne: Heinrich-Barth Institut, pp. 33–51.

Kopytoff, I. (1987). The Internal African Frontier: The Making of African Political Culture. In I. Kopytoff, ed., *The African Frontier: The Reproduction of Traditional African Societies*, Bloomington: Indiana University Press, pp. 3–84.

Kraemer, B., & Liszka, K. (2016). Evidence for Administration of the Nubian Fortresses in the Late Middle Kingdom: The Semna Dispatches. *Journal of Egyptian History*, **9**(1), 1–65.

Krishna, S. (1994). Cartographic Anxiety: Mapping the Body Politic in India. *Alternatives*, **19**(4), 507–521.

Kuhlmann, K. P. (2013). The Realm of "Two Deserts": Siwah Oasis between East and West. In F. Förster & H. Riemer, eds., *Desert Road Archaeology in Ancient Egypt and Beyond*, Cologne: Heinrich-Barth Institut, pp. 133–166.

Laakkonen, V. V. (2020). Borders as Practices and Processes. *Suomen Antropologi: Journal of the Finnish Anthropological Society*, **44**, 84–91.

Lakomy, K. C. (2016). *"Der Löwe auf dem Schlachtfeld": Das Grab KV 36 und die Bestattung des Maiherperi im Tal der Könige*, Wiesbaden: Reichert.

Landgráfová, R. (2011). *It Is My Good Name That You Should Remember: Egyptian Biographical Texts on Middle Kingdom Stelae*, Prague: Czech Institute of Egyptology.

Langer, C. (2018). The Concept of "Frontier" in New Kingdom Egypt: A Comparative Approach to the Spatiality of Ideology. In G. Chantrain & J. Winand, eds., *Time and Space at Issue in Ancient Egypt*, Hamburg: Widmaier, pp. 47–70.

Langer, C., & Fernández-Götz, M. (2020). Boundaries, Borders and Frontiers: Contemporary and Past Perspectives. *eTopoi Journal for Ancient Studies*, 7, 33–47.

Larsen, M. T., & Lassen, A. W. (2014). Cultural Exchange at Kültepe. In M. Kozuh, W. Henkelman, C. E. Jones, & C. Woods, eds., *Extraction and Control: Studies in Honor of Matthew W. Stolper*, Chicago, IL: Oriental Institute Press, pp. 171–188.

Lave, J., & Wenger, E. (1991). *Situated Learning: Legitimate Peripheral Participation*, Cambridge: Cambridge University Press.

Leahy, A. (1985). The Libyan Period in Egypt: An Essay in Interpretation. *Libyan Studies*, **16**, 51–65.

Lesko, L. H. (1996). Egyptian Wine Production during the New Kingdom. In P. McGovern, S. J. Fleming, & S. H. Katz, eds., *The Origins and Ancient History of Wine*, London: Routledge, pp. 245–261.

Li, P. S. (2004). Social Capital and Economic Outcomes for Immigrants and Ethnic Minorities. *Journal of International Migration and Integration*, **5**, 171–190.

Lichtheim, M. (1980). The Praise of Cities in the Literature of the Egyptian New Kingdom. In S. M. Burstein & L. A. Okin, eds., *Panhellenica: Essays in Ancient History and Historiography in Honor of Truesdell S. Brown*, Lawrence, KS: Coronado Press, pp. 15–23.

Lichtheim, M. (2006a). *Ancient Egyptian Literature: Volume I, The Old and Middle Kingdoms*, Berkeley: University of California Press.

Lichtheim, M. (2006b). *Ancient Egyptian Literature: Volume II, The New Kingdom*, Berkeley: University of California Press.

Lightfoot, E. (ed.). (2008). Movement, Mobility and Migration. *Archaeological Review from Cambridge*, **23**(2).

Lightfoot, K. G., & Martinez, A. (1995). Frontiers and Boundaries in Archaeological Perspective. *Annual Review of Anthropology*, **24**, 471–492.

Lightfoot, K. G., Schiff, A. M., & Martinez, A. (1998). Daily Practice and Material Culture in Pluralistic Social Settings: An Archaeological Study of Culture Change and Persistence from Fort Ross, California. *American Antiquity*, **63**, 199–222.

Lilyquist, C. (2003). *The Tomb of Three Foreign Wives of Tuthmosis III*, New York: Metropolitan Museum of Art.

Liszka, K. (2012). "We Have Come to Serve the Pharaoh": A Study of the Medjay and Pangrave as an Ethnic Group and as Mercenaries from c. 2300 BCE until c. 1050 BCE (PhD Thesis), University of Pennsylvania.

Liszka, K. (2015). Are the Bearers of the Pan-Grave Archaeological Culture Identical to the Medjay-People in the Egyptian Textual Record? *Journal of Ancient Egyptian Interconnections*, **7**(2), 42–60.

Liszka, K. (2022). Eight Medjay Walk into a Palace: Bireaucractic Categorization and Cultural Mistranslation of Peoples in Contact. In D. Candelora, N. Ben-Marzouk, & K. M. Cooney, eds., *Ancient Egyptian Society: Challenging Assumptions, Exploring Approaches*, London: Routledge, pp. 122–139.

Liverani, M. (1990). *Prestige and Interest: International Relations in the Near East ca. 1600–1100 BC*, Padua: Sargon SRL.

Liverani, M. (2001). Moving Borders. In M. Liverani, ed., *International Relations in the Ancient Near East, 1600–1100 BC*, London: Palgrave Macmillan, pp. 46–51.

Lloyd, A. B. (2007). Darius I in Egypt: Suez and Hibis. In C. Tuplin, ed., *Persian Responses: Political and Cultural Interaction with(in) the Achaemenid Empire*, Swansea: Classical Press of Wales, pp. 99–115.

Lohwasser, A. (2001). Queenship in Kush: Status, Role and Ideology of Royal Women. *Journal of the American Research Center in Egypt*, **38**, 61–76.

Loprieno, A. (1988). *Topos und Mimesis: Zum Ausländer in der ägyptischen Literatur*, Wiesbaden: Harrassowitz.

Loprieno, A. (2001). *La pensée et l'écriture: Pour une analyse sémiotique de la culture égyptienne. Quatre séminaires à l'École Pratique des Hautes Études. Section des Sciences religieuses, 25–27 mai 2000, Paris*, Paris: Cybele.

Lorton, D. (1974). *The Juridical Terminology of International Relations in Egyptian Texts through Dyn. XVIII*, Baltimore, MD: Johns Hopkins University Press.

Lorton, D. (1977). The Treatment of Criminals in Ancient Egypt: Through the New Kingdom. *Journal of the Economic and Social History of the Orient*, **20** (1), 2–64.

Lucy, S. (2005). Ethnic and Cultural Identities. In M. Díaz-Andreu, S. Lucy, S. Babic, & D. N. Edwards, eds., *The Archaeology of Identity: Approaches to Gender, Age, Status, Ethnicity and Religion*, London: Routledge, pp. 86–109.

Maran, J., & Stockhammer, P. W. (eds.). (2012). *Materiality and Social Practice: Transformative Capacities of Intercultural Encounters*, Oxford: Oxbow Books.

Mathieson, I., Bettles, E., Davies, S., & Smith, H. S. (1995). A Stela of the Persian Period from Saqqara. *Journal of Egyptian Archaeology*, **81**, 23–41.

Matić, U. (2020). *Ethnic Identities in the Land of the Pharaohs: Past and Present Approaches in Egyptology*, Cambridge: Cambridge University Press.

McDowell, A. G. (1999). *Village Life in Ancient Egypt: Laundry Lists and Love Songs*, New York: Oxford University Press.

Meurer, G. (1996). *Nubier in Ägypten bis zum Beginn des Neuen Reiches: Zur Bedeutung der Stele Berlin 14753*, Berlin: Achet.

Minor, E. J. (2012). The Use of Egyptian and Egyptianizing Material Culture in Nubian Burials of the Classic Kerma Period (PhD Dissertation), University of California, Berkeley.

Moeller, N. (2018). *The Archaeology of Urbanism in Ancient Egypt: From the Predynastic Period to the End of the Middle Kingdom*, Cambridge: Cambridge University Press.

Moers, G. (2005). Auch der Feind war nur ein Mensch: Kursorisches zu einer Teilansicht pharaonischer Selbst- und Fremdwahrnehmungsoperationen. In H. Felber, ed., *Feinde und Aufrührer. Konzepte von Gegnerschaft in ägyptischen Texten besonders des Mittleren Reiches*, Stuttgart: Verlag der Sächsischen Akademie der Wissenschaften, pp. 223–282.

Moers, G. (2010). The World and the Geography of Otherness in Pharaonic Egypt. In K. A. Raaflaub & R. J. A. Talbert, eds., *Geography and Ethnography: Perceptions of the World in Pre-modern Societies*, Oxford: Wiley-Blackwell, pp. 169–181.

Moers, G. (2015). "Egyptian Identity"? Unlikely, and Never National. In S. Uljas, H. Amstutz, A. Dorn, M. Müller, & M. Ronsdorf, eds., *Fuzzy Boundaries: Festschrift für Antonio Loprieno*, Hamburg: Widmaier, pp. 693–704.

Mojtahed-Zadeh, P. (2005). "Boundary" in Ancient Persian Tradition of Statehood: An Introduction to the Origins of the Concept of Boundary in Pre-modern History. *GeoJournal*, **62**(1), 51–58.

Moorey, P. R. S. (2001). The Mobility of Artisans and Opportunities for Technology Transfer between Western Asia and Egypt in the Late Bronze Age. In A. J. Shortland, ed., *The Social Context of Technological Change: Egypt and the Near East, 1650–1550 BC*, Oxford: Oxbow Books, pp. 1–14.

Moran, W. L. (1992). *The Amarna Letters*, Baltimore, MD: Johns Hopkins University Press.

Moreno García, J. C. (2015). Ḥwt jḥ(w)t: The Administration of the Western Delta and the "Libyan Question" in the 3rd Millennium. *Journal of Egyptian Archaeology*, **101**, 69–105.

Moreno García, J. C. (2024). Contact, Mobility, Migration: Social and Economic Interaction across Egyptian Borders (Early and Middle Bronze Age). In G. Miniaci, C. Greco, P. Del Vesco, M. Mancini, & C. Alù, eds., *Ancient Egypt and the Surrounding World: Contact, Trade, and Influence. Studies presented to Marilina Betrò*, Pisa: Pisa University Press, pp. 5–22.

Moreno García, J. C., & Schneider, T. (eds.). (2018). Ethnic Identities in Ancient Egypt and the Identity of Egyptology. *Journal of Egyptian History*, **11**, 241–244.

Morris, E. (2004). *The Architecture of Imperialism: Military Bases and the Evolution of Foreign Policy in Egypt's New Kingdom*, Leiden: Brill.

Morris, E. (2010a). Insularity and Island Identity in the Oases Bordering Egypt's Great Sand Sea. In S. Ikram & Z. A. Hawass, eds., *Thebes and Beyond: Studies in Honor of Kent R. Weeks*, Cairo: Conseil Suprême des Antiquités de l'Egypte, pp. 129–144.

Morris, E. (2010b). Opportunism in Contested Lands, BC and AD: Or How Abdi-Ashirta, Aziru, and Padsha Khan Zadran Got Away with Murder. In Z. A. Hawass & J. H. Wegner, eds., *Millions of Jubilees: Studies in Honor of David P. Silverman*, Vol. 1, Cairo: Conseil Suprême des Antiquités de l'Egypte, pp. 413–438.

Morris, E. (2014). Mitanni Enslaved: Prisoners of War, Pride, and Productivity in a New Imperial Regime. In J. Galán, B. Bryan, & P. Dorman, eds., *Creativity and Innovation in the Reign of Hatshepsut*, Chicago, IL: Oriental Institute Press, pp. 361–380.

Morris, E. (2017). Prevention through Deterrence along Egypt's Northeastern Border: Or the Politics of a Weaponized Desert. *Journal of Eastern Mediterranean Archaeology & Heritage Studies*, **5**(2), 133–147.

Mourad, A.-L. (2013). Asiatics and Abydos: From the Twelfth Dynasty to the Early Second Intermediate Period. *Bulletin of the Australian Centre for Egyptology*, **24**, 31–58.

Mourad, A.-L. (2015). *Rise of the Hyksos: Egypt and the Levant from the Middle Kingdom to the Early Second Intermediate Period*, Oxford: Archaeopress.

Mourad, A.-L. (2019). On Cultural Interference and the Egyptian Storm God. In M. Bietak & S. Prell, eds., *The Enigma of the Hyksos*, Vol. 1, Wiesbaden: Harrassowitz, pp. 225–237.

Mourad, A.-L. (2021). *The Enigma of the Hyksos Volume II: Transforming Egypt into the New Kingdom. The Impact of the Hyksos and Egyptian–Near Eastern Relations*, Gottingen: Harrassowitz.

Muhlestein, K. (2008). Execration Ritual. In J. Dieleman & W. Wendrich, eds., *UCLA Encyclopedia of Egyptology*, **1**(1). https://escholarship.org/uc/item/3f6268zf.

Müller, M. (2015). Modeling Household Identity in a Multi-ethnic Society. *Archaeological Review from Cambridge*, **30**(1), 102–112.

Müller-Wollermann, R. (1996). Gaugrenzen und Grenzstelen. *Chronique d'Egypte*, **71**(141), 5–16.

Mullin, D. (2011a). Border Crossings: The Archaeology of Borders and Borderlands. An Introduction. In *Places in Between: The Archaeology of Social, Cultural and Geographical Borders and Borderlands*, Oxford: Oxbow, pp. 1–12.

Mullin, D. (2011b). Towards an Archaeology of Borders and Borderlands. In *Places in Between: The Archaeology of Social, Cultural and Geographical Borders and Borderlands*, Oxford: Oxbow, pp. 99–104.

Murphy, A. B. (1996). The Sovereign State System as Political-Territorial Ideal: Historical and Contemporary Considerations. In T. J. Biersteker & C. Weber, eds., *State Sovereignty as Social Construct*, Cambridge: Cambridge University Press, pp. 81–120.

Murray, M. A. (2000). Viticulture and Wine Production. In P. T. Nicholson & I. Shaw, eds., *Ancient Egyptian Materials and Technology*, Cambridge: Cambridge University Press, pp. 577–608.

Naunton, C. (2010). Libyans and Nubians. In A. B. Lloyd, ed., *A Companion to Ancient Egypt*, Vol. 1, Malden, MA: Wiley, pp. 120–139.

Newberry, P. E. (1893). *Beni Hasan I*, London: Egypt Exploration Fund.

Newman, D. (2002). Citizenship, Identity and Location: The Changing Discourse of Israeli Geopolitics. In D. Atkinson & K. Dodds, eds., *Geopolitical Traditions: Critical Histories of a Century of Geopolitical Thought*, London: Routledge, pp. 302–331.

Newman, D. (2003). On Borders and Power: A Theoretical Framework. *Journal of Borderlands Studies*, **18**(1), 13–25.

O'Connor, D. (1987). The Nature of Tjemehu (Libyan) Society in the Late New Kingdom. In A. Leahy, ed., *Libya and Egypt, c. 1300–750 BC*, London: SOAS Centre of Near and Middle Eastern Studies and the Society for Libyan Studies, pp. 29–114.

O'Connor, D. (2003). Egypt's Views of "Others." In J. Tait, ed., *"Never Had the Like Occurred": Egypt's View of Its Past*, London: UCL Press, pp. 155–186.

O'Connor, D. (2012). From Topography to Cosmos: Ancient Egypt's Multiple Maps. In R. J. A. Talbert, ed., *Ancient Perspectives: Maps and Their Place in Mesopotamia, Egypt, Greece, and Rome*, Chicago, IL: University of Chicago Press, pp. 47–80.

Paasi, A. (2003). Region and Place: Regional Identity in Question. *Progress in Human Geography*, **27**(4), 475–485.

Paasi, A. (2013). Borders and Border-Crossings. In N. C. Johnson, R. H. Schein, & J. Winders, eds., *The Wiley-Blackwell Companion to Cultural Geography*, Malden, MA: Wiley, pp. 478–493.

Paasi, A. (2018). Borderless Worlds and Beyond: Challenging the State-Centric Cartographies. In A. Paasi, E.-K. Prokkola, J. Saarinen, & K. Zimmerbauer, eds., *Borderless Worlds for Whom?* London: Routledge, pp. 21–36.

Paasi, A. (2020). Problematizing "Bordering, Ordering, and Othering" as Manifestations of Socio-spatial Fetishism. *Tijdschrift Voor Economische En Sociale Geografie*, **112**(1), 18–25.

Paasi, A. (2022). Examining the Persistence of Bounded Spaces: Remarks on Regions, Territories, and the Practices of Bordering. *Geografiska Annaler: Series B, Human Geography*, **104**(1), 9–26.

Paasi, A., & Zimmerbauer, K. (2016). Penumbral Borders and Planning Paradoxes: Relational Thinking and the Question of Borders in Spatial Planning. *Environment and Planning A: Economy and Space*, **48**(1), 75–93.

Panagiotopoulos, D. (2012). Encountering the Foreign: (De-)constructing Alterity in the Archaeologies of the Bronze Age Mediterranean. In J. Maran & P. W. Stockhammer, eds., *Materiality and Social Practice: Transformative Capacities of Intercultural Encounters*, Oxford: Oxbow, pp. 51–60.

Pantalacci, L. (2013). Balat, a Frontier Town and Its Archive. In J. C. Moreno García, ed., *Ancient Egyptian Administration*, Leiden: Brill, pp. 197–214.

Parciack, R. (2018). Borderline Nationalism: Restructuring the Wagah–Attari Border "Retreat Ceremony" and Its Media Representations. *South Asia: Journal of South Asian Studies*, **41**(4), 744–762.

Parker, B. J. (2006). Toward an Understanding of Borderland Processes. *American Antiquity*, **71**(1), 77–100.

Parker, N., & Vaughan-Williams, N. (2009). Lines in the Sand? Towards an Agenda for Critical Border Studies. *Geopolitics*, **14**(3), 582–587.

Parkinson, R. B. (ed.). (2012). *The Tale of the Eloquent Peasant: A Reader's Commentary*, Hamburg: Widmaier.

Peirce, L. (2019). Foreigners at Karnak: Utilising the "Other" for the Study of Egyptian Identity from the Second Intermediate Period until the Reign of Thutmose III (c. 1803–1425 BC) (PhD Thesis), Macquarie University.

Philip, G. (2006). *Tell el-Dab'a XV: Metalwork and Metalworking Evidence of the Late Middle Kingdom and Second Intermediate Period*, Vienna: Österreichische Akademie der Wissenschaften.

Phinney, J. S., Horenczyk, G., Liebkind, K., & Vedder, P. (2001). Ethnic Identity, Immigration, and Well-Being: An Interactional Perspective. *Journal of Social Issues*, **57**(3), 493–510.

Pope, J. (2014). *Double Kingdom under Taharqo: Studies in the History of Kush and Egypt, c. 690–664 BC*, Leiden: Brill.

Priglinger, E. (2018). The Role of Migration Theory in Egyptology. *Journal of Ancient Egyptian Interconnections*, **19**, 22–42.

Priglinger, E. (2019). Different Aspects of Mobility and Migration during the Middle Kingdom. *Ägypten Und Levante*, **29**, 331–354.

Purewal, N. (2003). The Indo–Pak Border: Displacements, Aggressions and Transgressions. *Contemporary South Asia*, **12**(4), 539–556.

Quirke, S. (1988). Frontier or Border? The Northeast Delta in Middle Kingdom Texts. In *Proceedings of the Colloquium "The Archaeology, Geography and History of the Egyptian Delta in Pharaonic Times," Wadham College, Oxford, UK, 29–31 August 1988*, Eynsham: Cotswalds Press, pp. 261–275.

Ragazzoli, C. C. D. (2011). Why Did Ancient Egyptians Long for Their Cities? City, Nostalgia and Identity Fashioning in the New Kingdom. In E. Subías, P. Azara, J. Carruesco, I. Fiz, & R. Cuesta, eds., *The Space of the City in Graeco-Roman Egypt: Image and Reality*, Tarragona: Institut Català d'Arqueologia Clàssica.

Redford, D. B. (1992). *Egypt, Canaan, and Israel in Ancient Times*, Princeton, NJ: Princeton University Press.

Redmount, C. A. (1995). Ethnicity, Pottery, and the Hyksos at Tell El-Maskhuta in the Egyptian Delta. *The Biblical Archaeologist*, **58**(4), 182–190.

Ricketts, S. M. (2020). The Sheikh Muftah Cultural Unit: Insights into Social Relations with Old Kingdom Egyptians, Dakhleh Oasis and Desert Surrounds. In A. R. Warfe, J. C. R. Gill, C. R. Hamilton, A. J. Pettman, & D. A. Stewart, eds., *Dust, Demons and Pots: Studies in Honour of Colin A. Hope*, Leuven: Peeters, pp. 599–614.

Roccati, A. (2015). DUGURASU = rw-ḫꜣwt. In A. Archi & A. Bramanti, eds., *Tradition and Innovation in the Ancient Near East: Proceedings of the 57th Rencontre Assyriologique Internationale at Rome 4–8 July 2011*, Winona Lake, IN: Eisenbrauns, pp. 155–160.

Rothe, U. (2014). Ethnicity in the Roman Northwest. In J. McInerney, ed., *A Companion to Ethnicity in the Ancient Mediterranean*, London: Wiley, pp. 497–513.

Rudmin, F. W., Nilsen, C. V., & Olsen, B. R. (2007). Acculturation of the Majority Population: How Norwegians Adopt Minority Ways. *Psykologisk Tidsskrift*, **11**(3), 43–51.

Rudnicki, J. (2016). The Hans Island Dispute and the Doctrine of Occupation. *Studia Iuridica*, **68**, 307–320.

Russmann, E. R. (1995). Kushite Headdresses and "Kushite" Style. *Journal of Egyptian Archaeology*, **81**, 227–232.

Ryholt, K. S. B. (1997). *The Political Situation in Egypt during the Second Intermediate Period, c. 1800–1550 BC*, Copenhagen: Carsten Niebuhr Institute of Near Eastern Studies, University of Copenhagen; Museum Tusculanum Press.

Saretta, P. (2016). *Asiatics in Middle Kingdom Egypt: Perceptions and Reality*, London: Bloomsbury.

Säve-Söderbergh, T. (1949). A Buhen Stela from the Second Intermediate Period (Khartum No. 18). *Journal of Egyptian Archaeology*, **35**, 50–58.

Schenkel, W. (1965). *Memphis, Herakleopolis, Theben: Die epigraphischen Zeugnisse der 7. – 11. Dynastie Ägyptens*, Wiesbaden: Harrassowitz. https://doi.org/10.11588/diglit.17774.

Schlott-Schwab, A. (1981). *Die Ausmasse Ägyptens nach altägyptischen Texten*, Wiesbaden: Harrassowitz.

Schneider, T. (1992). *Asiatische Personennamen in ägyptischen Quellen des Neuen Reiches*, Gottingen: Saint-Paul.

Schneider, T. (2003). *Ausländer in Ägypten während des Mittleren Reiches und der Hyksoszeit II: Die ausländische Bevölkerung*, Wiesbaden: Harrassowitz.

Schneider, T. (2006). Akkulturation – Identität – Elitekultur: Eine Positionsbestimmung zur Frage der Existenz und des Status von Ausländern in der Elite des Neuen Reiches. In R. Gundlach & A. Klug, eds., *Der Ägyptische Hof des Neuen Reiches: Seine Gesellschaft und Kultur im Spannungsfeld zwischen Innen- und Außenpolitik*, Wiesbaden: Harrassowitz, pp. 201–216.

Schneider, T. (2008). Fremdwörter in der ägyptischen Militärsprache des Neuen Reiches und ein Bravourstück des Elitesoldaten (Pap. Anastasi I 23, 2–7). *Journal of the Society for the Study of Egyptian Antiquities*, **35**, 181–205.

Schneider, T. (2010). Foreigners in Egypt. In W. Wendrich, ed., *Egyptian Archaeology*, Chichester: Wiley-Blackwell, pp. 143–163.

Schneider, T. (2011). Wie der Wettergott Ägypten aus der großen Flut errettete: Ein "inkulturierter" ägyptischer Sintflut-Mythos und die Gründung der Ramsesstadt. *Journal of the Society for the Study of Egyptian Antiquities*, **38**, 173–193.

Schneider, T. (2017). Horus Is Watching You: Surveillance. In M. E. Babej, ed., *Yesterday – Tomorrow: A Work in Aspective Realism*, Heidelberg: Kehrer, pp. 95–101.

Sethe, K. (1927). *Erläuterungen zu den ägyptischen Lesestücken: Texte der Mittleren Reiches*, Leipzig: Hinrichs.

Sethe, K. (1932). *Urkunden des Alten Reiches*, Vol. I, Leipzig: Hinrichs.

Sethe, K. (1961). *Urkunden der 18. Dynastie*, Vol. IV:8, Berlin: Akademie.

Shachar, A. (2019). Bordering Migration/Migrating Borders. *Berkeley Journal of International Law*, **37**(1), 93–147.

Shaw, I. (ed.). (2012). *Ancient Egyptian Technology and Innovation: Transformations in Pharaonic Material Culture*, London: Bloomsbury.

Shennan, S. (ed.). (1989). *Archaeological Approaches to Cultural Identity*, London: Unwin Hyman.

Shore, A. F. (1987). Egyptian Cartography. In J. B. Harley & D. Woodward, eds., *A History of Cartography: Cartography in Prehistoric, Ancient, and Medieval Europe and the Mediterranean*, Vol. 1, Chicago, IL: University of Chicago Press, pp. 117–129.

Siegel, O. (2022). Reevaluating the Role of Inter-polity Boundaries (tȝšw) in Middle and New Kingdom Egypt. *Journal of Egyptian History*, **15**(1), 1–42.

Siegel, O. (2024). Monumental Walls, Sovereign Power and Value(s) in Pharaonic Egypt. *Cambridge Archaeological Journal*, **34**(3), 439–452.

Simpson, W. K. (ed.). (2003). *The Literature of Ancient Egypt: An Anthology of Stories, Instructions, Stelae, Autobiographies, and Poetry*, New Haven, CT: Yale University Press.

Smith, D. M. (2016). Introduction: The Sharing and Dividing of Geographical space. In M. Chisholm & D. M. Smith, eds., *Shared Space: Divided Space*, London: Routledge, pp. 1–21.

Smith, M. L. (2005). Networks, Territories, and the Cartography of Ancient States. *Annals of the Association of American Geographers*, **95**(4), 832–849.

Smith, M. L. (2007). Territories, Corridors, and Networks: A Biological Model for the Premodern State. *Complexity*, **12**(4), 28–35.

Smith, S. T. (1991). Askut and the Role of the Second Cataract Forts. *Journal of the American Research Center in Egypt*, **28**, 107–132.

Smith, S. T. (1995). *Askut in Nubia: The Economics and Ideology of Egyptian Imperialism in the Second Millennium BC*, London: Kegan Paul International.

Smith, S. T. (1997). State and Empire in the Middle and New Kingdom. In J. Lustig, ed., *Anthropology and Egyptology: A Developing Dialogue*, Sheffield: Sheffield Academic Press, pp. 66–89.

Smith, S. T. (2003). *Wretched Kush: Ethnic Identities and Boundaries in Egypt's Nubian Empire*, London: Routledge.

Smith, S. T. (2005). To the Supports of Heaven: Political and Ideological Concepts of Frontiers in Ancient Egypt. In B. J. Parker & L. Rodseth, eds.,

In Untaming the Frontier in Anthropology, Archaeology, and History, Tucson: University of Arizona Press, pp. 207–237.

Smith, S. T. (2007). Ethnicity and Culture. In T. Wilkinson, ed., *The Egyptian World*, London: Routledge, pp. 218–241.

Smith, S. T. (2013). Revenge of the Kushites: Assimilation and Resistance in Egypt's New Kingdom Empire and Nubian Ascendancy over Egypt. In G. Areshian, ed., *Empires and Complexity: On the Crossroads of Archaeology*, Los Angeles, CA: Cotsen Institute of Archaeology Press, pp. 84–107.

Smith, S. T., & Buzon, M. R. (2018). Cross-Cultural Interaction in the Ancient Egyptian and Nubian Borderland. In U. M. Green & K. E. Costion, eds., *Modeling Cross-Cultural Interaction in Ancient Borderlands*, Gainesville: University Press of Florida, pp. 89–113.

Smither, P. C. (1945). The Semnah Despatches. *Journal of Egyptian Archaeology*, **31**(1), 3–10.

Spalinger, A. J. (1979). Some Notes on the Libyans of the Old Kingdom and Later Historical Reflexes. *Journal of the Society for the Study of Egyptian Antiquities*, **9**, 125–160.

Stantis, C., & Schutkowski, H. (2019). Stable Isotope Analyses to Investigate Hyksos Identity and Origins. In M. Bietak & S. Prell, eds., *The Enigma of the Hyksos Vol. I, ASOR Conference Boston 2017 – ICAANE Conference Munich 2018 – Proceedings*, Vienna: Austrian Academy of Sciences Press, pp. 321–338.

Stockhammer, P. W. (2012a). Conceptualizing Cultural Hybridization in Archaeology. In P. W. Stockhammer, ed., *Conceptualizing Cultural Hybridization: A Transdisciplinary Approach*, Heidelberg: Springer, pp. 43–58.

Stockhammer, P. W. (2012b). Performing the Practice Turn in Archaeology. *Journal of Transcultural Studies*, **3**(1), 7–42.

Strassoldo, R. (1977). The Study of Boundaries. *Jerusalem Journal of International Relations*, **2**(3), 81–107.

Tallet, P. (2009). Les Égyptiens et le littoral de la mer Rouge à l'époque pharaonique. *Comptes rendus des séances de l'Académie des Inscriptions et Belles-Lettres*, **153**(2), 687–719.

Tallet, P. (2020). Glimpses on the Early Cult of Seth in Dakhleh Oasis. In A. R. Warfe, J. C. R. Gill, C. R. Hamilton, A. J. Pettman, & D. A. Stewart, eds., *Dust, Demons and Pots: Studies in Honour of Colin A. Hope*, Leuven: Peeters, pp. 705–714.

Tarawneh, H. (2011). Amarna Letters: Two Languages, Two Dialogues. In J. Mynářová, ed., *Egypt and the Near East – The Crossroads: Proceedings of an International Conference on the Relations of Egypt and the Near East in the Bronze Age, Prague, September 1–3, 2010*, Prague: Czech Institute of Egyptology, pp. 271–284.

Taterka, F. (2024). "You Were Strangers in the Land of Egypt" (Exod 22:20): Notes on the Attitude(s) towards Foreigners in Ancient Egypt. *The Biblical Annals*, **14**(71/1), 115–146.

Terlouw, K. (2009). Rescaling Regional Identities: Communicating Thick and Thin Regional Identities. *Studies in Ethnicity and Nationalism*, **9**(3), 452–464.

Thum, J. (2022). Sensing Salience in the Landscapes of Egyptian Royal Living-Rock Stelae. In K. Neumann & A. Thomason, eds., *The Routledge Handbook of the Senses in the Ancient Near East*, Oxford: Routledge, pp. 267–296.

Török, L. (2008). *Between Two Worlds: The Frontier Region between Ancient Nubia and Egypt 3700 BC–500 AD*, Leiden: Brill.

Uphill, E. (1967). The Nine Bows. *Journal of the Ancient Near Eastern Society "Ex Oriente Lux,"* **19**, 393–420.

Vallet, E. (2022). State of Border Walls in a Globalized World. In A. Bissonnette & E. Vallet, eds., *Borders and Border Walls: In-security, Symbolism, Vulnerabilities*, London: Routledge, pp. 7–24.

Valloggia, M. (1985). Les amiraux de l'oasis de Dakhleh. In F. Geus & E. Thill, eds., *Mélanges offerts à Jean Vercoutter*, Paris: Éditions Recherche sur les Civilisations, pp. 355–364.

Van den Brink, E. C. M., & Levy, T. (eds.). (2002). *Egypt and the Levant: Interrelations from the 4th through the Early 3rd Millennium BCE*, London: Leicester University Press.

Van Houtum, H., & Van Naerssen, T. (2002). Bordering, Ordering and Othering. *Tijdschrift Voor Economische En Sociale Geografie*, **93**(2), 125–136.

Van Pelt, W. P. (2013). Revising Egypto–Nubian Relations in New Kingdom Lower Nubia: From Egyptianization to Cultural Entanglement. *Cambridge Archaeological Journal*, **23**(3), 523–550.

Vigo, M. (2024). The Hittite–Egyptian Relations before the Amarna Age: Notes on KBo 31.40 and Related Texts. In G. Miniaci, C. Greco, P. Del Vesco, M. Mancini, & C. Alù, eds., *Ancient Egypt and the Surrounding World: Contact, Trade, and Influence. Studies Presented to Marilina Betrò*, Pisa: Pisa University Press, pp. 121–136.

Vogel, C. (2011). This Far and Not a Step Further! The Ideological Concept of Ancient Egyptian Boundary Stelae. In S. Bar, D. Kahn, & J. Shirley, eds., *Egypt, Canaan and Israel: History, Imperialism, Ideology and Literature*, Leiden: Brill, pp. 320–341.

Wendrich, W. (ed.). (2012). *Archaeology and Apprenticeship: Body Knowledge, Identity, and Communities of Practice*, Tucson: University of Arizona Press.

Wenger, E. (1998). *Communities of Practice: Learning, Meaning, and Identity*, Cambridge: Cambridge University Press.

Wengrow, D. (2006). *The Archaeology of Early Egypt: Social Transformations in North-East Africa, 10,000 to 2,650 BC: Social Transformations in North-East Africa, c. 10,000 to 2,650 BC*, Cambridge: Cambridge University Press.

Wente, E. F. (ed.). (1990). *Letters from Ancient Egypt*. (E. S. Meltzer, Trans.), Atlanta, GA: Scholars Press.

White, R. (1991). *The Middle Ground: Indians, Empires, and Republics in the Great Lakes Region, 1650–1815*, Cambridge: Cambridge University Press.

White, R. (2006). Creative Misunderstandings and New Understandings. *The William and Mary Quarterly*, **63**(1), 9–14.

Winand, J. (2017). Identifying Semitic Loanwords in Late Egyptian. In E. Grossman, P. Dils, T. S. Richter, & W. Schenkel, eds., *Greek Influence on Egyptian-Coptic: Contact-Induced Change in an Ancient African Language*, Hamburg: Widmaier. pp. 481–511.

Zibelius-Chen, K. (1988). *Die ägyptische Expansion nach Nubien: Eine Darlegung der Grundfaktoren*, Wiesbaden: Reichert.

Zivie, A. (2014). Le vizir et père du dieu 'Aper-El ('Abdiel). In G. Vittozzi, ed., *Egyptian Curses. I. Proceedings of the Egyptological Day Held at the National Research Council of Italy (CNR), Rome, 3rd December 2012, in the International Conference "Reading Catastrophes,"* Rome: Istituto di studi sul Mediterraneo antico, pp. 83–99.

Zivie-Coche, C. (2018). Les dieux des autres: Réception et identité dans le polythéisme égyptien. *Studi e Materiali Di Storia Delle Religioni*, **84**(1), 23–49.

Cambridge Elements

Ancient Egypt in Context

Gianluca Miniaci
University of Pisa

Gianluca Miniaci is Associate Professor in Egyptology at the University of Pisa, Honorary Researcher at the Institute of Archaeology, UCL – London, and Chercheur associé at the École Pratique des Hautes Études, Paris. He is currently co-director of the archaeological mission at Zawyet Sultan (Menya, Egypt). His main research interest focuses on the social history and the dynamics of material culture in Middle Bronze Age Egypt and its interconnections between the Levant, Aegean, and Nubia.

Juan Carlos Moreno García
CNRS, Paris

Juan Carlos Moreno García (PhD in Egyptology, 1995) is a CNRS senior researcher at the Sorbonne University, as well as lecturer on social and economic history of ancient Egypt at the École des Hautes Études en Sciences Sociales (EHESS) in Paris. He has published extensively on the administration, socio-economic history, and landscape organization of ancient Egypt, usually in a comparative perspective with other civilizations of the ancient world, and has organized several conferences on these topics.

Anna Stevens
University of Cambridge and Monash University

Anna Stevens is a research archaeologist with a particular interest in how material culture and urban space can shed light on the lives of the non-elite in ancient Egypt. She is Senior Research Associate at the McDonald Institute for Archaeological Research and Assistant Director of the Amarna Project (both University of Cambridge).

About the Series

The aim of this Elements series is to offer authoritative but accessible overviews of foundational and emerging topics in the study of ancient Egypt, along with comparative analyses, translated into a language comprehensible to non-specialists. Its authors will take a step back and connect ancient Egypt to the world around, bringing ancient Egypt to the attention of the broader humanities community and leading Egyptology in new directions.

Cambridge Elements

Ancient Egypt in Context

Elements in the Series

The Nile: Mobility and Management
Judith Bunbury and Reim Rowe

The Archaeology of Egyptian Non-Royal Burial Customs in New Kingdom Egypt and Its Empire
Wolfram Grajetzki

Power and Regions in Ancient States
Gary M. Feinman and Juan Carlos Moreno García

Ancient Egypt in Its African Context: Economic Networks, Social and Cultural Interactions
Andrea Manzo

Egyptian Archaeology and the Twenty-First-Century Museum
Alice Stevenson

Technology and Culture in Pharaonic Egypt: Actor Network Theory and the Archaeology of Things and People
Martin Fitzenreiter

Famine and Feast in Ancient Egypt
Ellen Morris

Hieroglyphs, Pseudo-Scripts and Alphabets: Their Use and Reception in Ancient Egypt and Neighbouring Regions
Ben Haring

Scribal Culture in Ancient Egypt
Niv Allon and Hana Navratilova

Making Memories in Ancient Egypt
Leire Olabarria

Monarchies and the Organization of Power: Ancient Egypt and Babylonia Compared (2100–1750 BC)
Juan Carlos Moreno García and Seth Richardson

Immigration and Borders in Ancient Egypt
Danielle Candelora

A full series listing is available at: www.cambridge.org/AECE

For EU product safety concerns, contact us at Calle de José Abascal, 56–1°,
28003 Madrid, Spain or eugpsr@cambridge.org.

www.ingramcontent.com/pod-product-compliance
Lightning Source LLC
LaVergne TN
LVHW011852060526
838200LV00054B/4294